HOW TO DO EVERYTHING RIGHT
AND LIVE TO REGRET IT

How to Do Everything Right and Live to Regret It

True Confessions of a Christian Woman

FAY ANGUS

1817

Harper & Row, Publishers, San Francisco

Cambridge, Hagerstown, New York, Philadelphia
London, Mexico City, São Paulo, Sydney

FIRST EDITION

Designer: Jim Mennick
Illustrator: Corbin Hillam

Library of Congress Cataloging in Publication Data

Angus, Fay.
    HOW TO DO EVERTHING RIGHT AND LIVE TO REGRET IT.
    1. Christian life—Anecdotes, facetiae, satire, etc.
2. Angus, Fay. I. Title.
BV4517.A53 1983   248.4   82–48425
ISBN 0–06–060236–8

---

83 84 85 86 87 10 9 8 7 6 5 4 3 2 1

To Richard Armour—
who needs to admit
that it really all started with Adam
&
To Even—
a most thoroughly misunderstood woman

Contents

Acknowledgments

Dr. Robert Vander Zaag, my pastor, who besides being marvelously good looking, taught me most of what I know about the sovereignty of God, the necessity of making midcourse corrections, and how to grow a choice cauliflower.

John Angus, my husband, who says *he* is the one who is marvelously good looking and, unless I acknowledge it, I may not live to regret it!

Anne and *Ian*, my children, who assure me that they are doing everything right, so I don't have to keep asking.

Roy M. Carlisle, my editor at Harper & Row San Francisco, who insisted that I write it right.

Lois Curley, my agent, who managed to tickle the muse in all the right places.

How to Do Everything Right & Live to Regret It

God knows, I tried!

To do everything right, that is. Whether I tried too hard, or not hard enough, depends upon whether you are me looking up at God, or God looking down at me, but whatever . . . I ended up in a series of dithers that smudged themselves all over the best of my intentions, many of which blot their way through the ink in this book.

From the time I could talk, I tried to talk right. Elocution was stressed as a vital part of my education, and the sisters at the Convent of the Sacred Heart did their part by poking me every time I used "me" instead of "I," and said "seen" instead of "saw." They determined that the vowels and consonants of the rain in Spain fell very precisely on my plain with an articulation of the Queen's English that would have done Professor Higgins proud.

From the time I could walk, I tried to walk right. "Shoulders back, spine straight, and best foot forward." Nobody bothered, however, to tell me which was my best foot—which may be one of the reasons I had a tendency to trip over myself as well as other people. This led to my enrollment in ballet school, where the *maîtress de rigour* made very sure that both feet became my best.

From time to time she would also tap my rib cage and say, "Pull up, Fay, you're sagging!" All my vertebrae would snap to rigid attention, and I discovered at an early age that the backbone in developing quality of deportment began by developing quality of backbone.

For the first ten years of my life family snapshots show me looking as though, like Socrates, I had marbles in my mouth (actually, they were gum balls). The butterfly bows that held my curls in two knobs on the top of my head looked as though they were deliberately tied too tight in an effort to stretch me up an extra notch or two (which they were).

In my teenage years, Fair-try Ferris taught me mathematics. He was a large man with a raucous laugh, who handed out assignments and weekly tests with inordinate glee. He would peer over his wire-rimmed glasses and bellow, "Now give it a *fair-try*, that's all I ask!"

He was fond of saying such unsettling things as, "If at first you don't succeed, try, try again!" Whereas I was prone to say, "If at first you don't succeed, why bother?"

I soon found out that the problem with mathematics is that if everything is not done exactly right, it is done completely wrong. This means a *fair-try* is not fair at all, especially for anyone who is earnestly trying.

Fair-try's hero was Robert Bruce.

"Think of him," he would say, "battle weary and sick with discouragement, lying on a bed of straw as he watched a spider try to swing a web across the beams of the cottage ceiling. . . ." Six times the spider failed—on the seventh try he made it.

"I, too, will try again," said Bruce. He did, and trounced the English at the bloody battle of Bannockburn, which the English did not think was fair at all.

I was never quite sure what all that had to do with πr^2, but in mathematics, on both my seventh and eighth tries, I flunked.

"Fall in love with whomever you like," my mother told me, "but for heaven's sake marry right. It is just as easy to marry someone sensible as not, and you certainly don't want your children to be utter twits!"

I fell in love with a lot of people I liked, most of whom my mother didn't, and not many were sensible. But I did marry right—or so my husband likes to tell me.

From a bloodline remotely related to Robert Bruce, he makes a fetish of the seventh try, and tries hard enough for both of us. The problem is, I have to live through the first, second, and third through sixth tries, which usually means holding the flashlight under the kitchen sink while he tries to fix the plumbing, or steadying the ladder as he tinkers with the wiring in the attic.

At times like that, it is not so much that I regret his trying to do things right, but rather his insistence on trying to do *everything,* right or wrong! When we get the plumber's bill and the electrician's bill, having spent the weekend either without water or in total darkness, my regret turns to sobbing remorse.

I have now posted on our refrigerator door, "if at first you don't succeed, call an expert."

To further prove that I married right, my husband bought a plaque of the Angus coat of arms, which he proudly hung in a prominent place in our entry hall.

It shows a strong arm holding a bow, framed by a thick black belt with a gold buckle. Emblazoned across the top is written in Gaelic, "Fortitude is Virtue," which is a Scottish interpretation of "Bite the Bullet."

Every time we have a family row, my husband rubs this motto, like a talisman. He tells me that it does not ensure that our children won't be twits, but it does ensure that at least his bloodline (if not mine) will give him (if not me) the endurance to cope with them if they are.

In trying to do everything right, this time by upholding the traditions of the family crest, I decided to build some fortitude into my son's virtue that would help give him a feeling for his heritage. On his tenth birthday I bought him an Angus tartan tie, a thick black belt with a gold buckle, and a bow and arrow. I told him to go outside and develop a strong arm.

Now it might have been perfectly all right for Henry Wadsworth Longfellow to shoot an arrow into the air and have it fall to earth he knew not where, but in our neighborhood people are very sticky about accountability, especially when it comes to arrows and other airborne projectiles.

"Under no circumstances are you to shoot it outside our yard, or up into the trees," I cautioned.

"But then we won't have enough range," my son grumbled, as his friend Bobby twanged the bow.

"Well . . ." I said thoughtfully, "I suppose you can stand in our driveway and aim towards the bushes, but only in our own wilderness area."

We live in a wilderness area. This is a nice way of saying that the frontage along our street has not been weeded, trimmed, or husbanded by the various husbands on our street for years and years, which gives it the look of the Garden of Eden after the curse.

I brought in the cat and dog and stayed safely under the protective covering of my own roof as the arrows went whizzing by.

Within a few minutes, a police car pulled into the driveway.

Bobby, being somewhat streetwise and knowing the ramifications of being caught with the evidence, handed my son all the arrows, put his hands in his pockets, looked down demurely, and whistled.

"Do you know that you are in possession of dangerous weapons?" asked the cop, counting the arrows my son was holding and pulling out his little yellow pad.

"Nope," said my son.

"Where did you get these?" asked the cop.

"From my Mom," said my son.

"I want to talk to your mother," said the cop.

"Sure—come on up," said my son.

"You tell her to come on down," snapped the cop.

What followed was ten minutes of verbal fortitude on the part of the cop, the like of which was enough to crumble the virtue of Robert Bruce himself. This gave me a disposition to thumb my nose at heraldry as I passed it hanging in our entry hall, and mutter unspeakable things under my breath, in neoclassical Gaelic.

That night at dinner I suggested that we augment the family coat of arms with a biblical motto—perhaps a scriptural version of "Fortitude is Virtue," where the only dangerous weapon would be the sword of the Spirit which is the word of God, and I would like to see any cop tangle with that!

At the time, our adult Sunday School class was studying an excellent exposé of Dungeons and Dragons—the book of Revelation. Coming complete with candlesticks, seals that needed breaking, Gog, Magog, Leviathan, and a beast with seven heads rising up out of the sea, its prophetic forebodings are enough to curdle the most fortitudinous of virtuous blood.

Fortunately, good triumphs over evil and the faithful get to rejoice at the marriage feast of the Lamb, which is a great relief.

Angelic choirs sing, "Blessings and glory, and wisdom and thanksgiving, and honor, and power, and might, be unto our God for ever and ever ..." to which we all can shout an enthusiastic *amen!*

It is heraldry that heralds the most magnificent of all—Maranatha, the Lord cometh!

Having long considered wishy-washy to be one of the cardinal sins, I suggested that we take as our spiritual motto, "Hot or cold, but never lukewarm!" (Revelation 3:15–16).

"Just think," I said, "it is applicable to tea, lemonade, porridge, meat and potatoes, political opinions, spiritual convictions, and showers—all inclusive!"

"Harumph," said my husband, "we're liable to burn our tongues, get hot under the collar, be called a bunch of hotheads, and have someone slam us into the cooler."

Then, giving a pathetic little sigh, he added, "Isn't there something like, 'In peace and quietness is my strength'?"

"Nope," I said. "There is, 'Thou shalt keep him in perfect peace whose mind is stayed on thee' (Isaiah 26:3), and, 'In quietness and in confidence shall be your strength' (Isaiah 30:15), but not peace and quietness together."

"Well, then there should be!" he said impatiently.

"Harumph!" I said.

To push my point, several days later I served up a lukewarm meal. The water was lukewarm, the soup lukewarm, the mashed potatoes, fried chicken, vegetables, and even the jello cubes, sloshing disgustingly around the bowl, were lukewarm.

"Ptui!" spluttered my son, dribbling a mouthful of water all over the lace tablecloth, "I need an ice cube."

"Ah-ha," I gloated, now you know what God feels

like: 'I would that thou wert cold or hot—so then, because thou art lukewarm, and neither cold nor hot, I will spew thee out of my mouth.'"

Red hot is the commitment that sparks the derring-do of faith lived in the active tense.

It pulls us out of the lethargy of casual complacency, and although it occasionally takes us where angels fear to tread, nevertheless, it takes us.

Faith is a verb—it moves.

Sometimes agonizingly slowly!

"My spiritual life advances with all the alacrity of an arthritic snail," a friend wrote. "I crawl onwards, inch by inch, blinking in unaccustomed light."

I thought of C. S. Lewis. "Now that I am a Christian," he said, "I do have moods in which the whole thing looks very improbable, but when I was an atheist I had moods in which Christianity looked terribly probable."

"Keep on crawling along," I wrote my friend. He did, through the quagmire of doubt and depression, until at last he was astonished by the powerful response of God to his stuttered confession, "Lord, I believe—help thou my unbelief!"

Heaven moved.

It moved him out of a hospital bed and into a reconstructed life.

Faith may not do everything right, but it dares to do.

It dares to ask the controversial question, "Why?" It dares to admit the equally controversial answer, "I don't know!" It sallies forth with a determination to slice truth from error; it wrestles down the elusive and the enigmatic . . . until it flames the soul in a red-hot passion of conviction that burns away immobile, insipid indifference.

In my poetry writing days, I attended monthly meetings with a group of local poets.

We deliberately chose to ruffle one another's creative feathers and we went through many a molting process in order to plume the qualitative productivity of trying to write things right.

I was the youngest in the bunch, which was rather a nice feeling. It is a considerable shock to find that nowadays I am frequently among the oldest in the bunch! I am finding out with some relief, however, that this too can be rather a nice feeling, especially when the youngest in the bunch turns to me and says, "What do *you* think?"

We met in the basement of the library, around a table pushed to one side in a labyrinth of books and stacks of outdated magazines. We talked over our work as the ghosts of writers past listened from their dusty shelves. Every once in a while, caught up with a burst of nostalgia, we would pick up an old book and quote a few lines. We realized with pertinent self-application that even the best pass through prime-time popularity and are all too soon gathering dust with yesterday.

The poet's pen probes deep into caverns of the heart—it scrapes away at the very bedrock of human emotions and writes in life-blood. Poets are never wishy-washy, seldom cold, and nearly always red hot!

Esther Webb was a red-hot poet.

She had spent most of her career as a Professor of English at Iowa Wesleyan College. She retired into the snug, almost obscure foothills of Sierra Madre, California, affectionately referred to by canyon folk as our oasis from insanity.

Esther may have nestled into our oasis, but in no way would she put up with snug obscurity. A spry seventy-five, with a mind sharp as a nettle, she continued to be a prolific writer. Her pen had a pitch that frequently rocked our boat.

Tall and gangly, she wore sweaters, even through much of the sweltering California heat. Her hands rustled papers with quick familiarity and her eye was trained to dart through pages searching for that special twist of words that puts excitement into the English language. When she found them, she would tilt back her head, rock on the hind legs of her chair, and smile with satisfaction, "Now, *that* is good!"

Esther never settled for a *fair-try*, she went for only the best!

The clarity of her thoughts had an impact on my life. She gave me many a "word in due season." They cling, like barnacles firmly attached to the hull of memory.

"Dare to discuss, dare to dispute. Dare to develop a different point of view. Dare to try—dare to fail. Dare to put a courage to your convictions that will raise you above the dead level of average."

"One man (woman) with courage makes a majority," she would say, quoting Andrew Jackson. "Make your life that majority of one, because strangely soon, life stops!"

I was just over the hump of thirty, grappling with toddlers and prey to the tyranny of chronic exhaustion. Far from thinking about the possibility of life stopping, the mundane routines that pilfered my time made me wonder if and when life would ever really start!

Esther was just what I needed—me, she probably could have done without.

One day she read aloud her "Portrait of a Woman." It changed my life.

It still haunts me, like Scrooge and his Ghost of Christmas Yet to Come, and apprehension wrings my heart. I use it, like a mirror, to see if year by passing year in any way it is beginning to reflect my face. Then it drives me on to renewed vigor.

> She has walked circumspectly all her days
>   cautioned her feet against snow-hidden ice
>   clutched guard-rails, dared no dangerous roads
>   avoided climbing rocks toward mountain tops.
>
> She has walked circumspectly all her days
>   thwarted the impulse to crash chairs to bits
>   kept tongue from lashing men's stupidity
>   restrained caresses, whispered no fervent words.
>
> Now, old, she sits in her one-windowed room
>   piecing together blocks for patchwork quilts
>   measuring time, her careful days stretched out
>   a waste of sterile, cold serenity.

A one-windowed room may have a pleasant view, patchwork is pretty, and serenity stretched out sounds exactly right, but . . .

"Please, O God, not cold and sterile wasted days!"

"Flame my soul red-hot with the courage of a conviction that will make my life a majority of one," I prayed. "Help me whisper fervent words, unleash my caresses. Let me stumble over the rocks on mountain paths, and slip and skid, but pick me up and push me on. Redeem my time, and let me risk the dare to do, in derring-do. Infect my sterile days with a rage to live, and a rage to give . . . my utmost . . . and then more."

I have never crashed a chair to bits.

"At $69.95 each, please don't," my husband said; but he added that it would be perfectly all right to bash my fist down on the dining room table once in a while, provided I did it very carefully so as not to rattle the cups and slop his tea.

My tongue has all too often lashed stupidity— most frequently my own! Now I search for fervent words.

"What is your most fervent word?" I asked my husband, as we watched the evening news.

"Chocolate, as in chocolate pudding," he said, as he finished off the last in his bowl and licked the spoon.

"Good heavens," I replied. "Mine is ecstasy, as in 'you are my ecstasy!'"

"Good heavens," he said, as he turned off the set.

That portrait of a woman moved me out from a

tap-polishing, drawer-lining, tissue-folding circumspection, to the accelerated pace of ring-around-the-bathtub and the comfortable clutter of ordered chaos that is often the fallout of faith lived in the active tense.

Red-hot conviction does not necessarily mean that we become foot-stomping, back-whomping, Bible-thumping believers (though God knows, I am!).

It does mean that we become the glove into which the hand of God will fit—passively available to do his active will.

It does mean obedience.

When I was in my early twenties, I applied for a job at a rather prestigious organization. The personnel questionnaire was long, and my experience was short.

Finally, I made it up through a series of interviews to one with the man who was vice-president, whose assistant I would become.

"Are you any good with figures?" he asked.

"No," I had to admit, somewhat shakily, and he looked disappointed.

"But," I added brightly, "I am rather good at doing *exactly* what I'm told!"

He smiled. I got the job! Obedience paid off.

Faith in the active tense is singing through the doldrums, or cheerfully tackling a humdrum task to bathe the commonplace with the radiance of a job well done.

It may even mean stifling a moan in the middle of the night, and a pillow wet with loneliness as soggy prayers palpate a heart numb with desperation. For some, faith lived in the active tense is simply fear that has the courage to keep moving forward.

Mother Angelica, the Roman Catholic nun who responded to what she calls the miracles of opportunity that God placed in her life and founded the Eternal Word Television Network, describes her faith as ". . . one foot on the ground and one foot in the air, and that queasy feeling in your stomach."

Called a woman of great faith, she says, "No. I'm not a woman of great faith; I'm a coward that keeps moving."

At age fifty-nine she is moving a monthly budget of $2.5 million through the RCA satellite Satcom, which budget she holds together by her dependence on divine guidance and providence.

"Do anything but just sit there and be a sponge," she says.

Hot or cold, but never lukewarm?

Make mine hot!

Adam & EveN,
God's Complement to Man

EveN in Eden

In the beginning, God created man. He took a long hard look and said, "Boy, this guy sure could use some help!"

Enter Eve, God's complement to man. She was a new and improved model of creation, with no whiskers, more curves, and, best of all, indoor plumbing.

Posturing an early narcissus complex, man promptly appropriated the complement toward himself and named her "wo-man." This gives rise to a lot of speculation as to what might have happened to the course of history had he named her something else—"aspidistra," for example. As it was, she had no choice in the matter but to tag along as the prefix to his ego, not only as the *"wo"* in *wo*man, but also as the *"fe"* in *fe*male.

Her first impulse was to go home to mother, but then she realized that she had no mother to go home to.

"Adam," she said, "I have a bone to pick with you!"

"Madam," said Adam, rubbing his ribs, "you already have!"

That became the first of many bones of contention between them, and was the root of such ominous expressions as, "I feel it in my bones," "Make no bones about it," and "You're nothing but a bone-head."

As the bone of his bone and flesh of his flesh, woman was made from man, for man. God could have made a man from man, for man and thus developed a totally hu*man* race . . . Adam and *B*ruce, followed perhaps by *C*harles, *D*aniel, *E*gbert, *F*rederick, and so on and so forth through all the letters of the alphabet.

Of course, just how Adam and Bruce would have birthed their genealogy is a matter for serious scientific conjecture, but it would have eliminated such sticky wickets as "discrimination on account of sex." For that matter, it would have eliminated the word "sex" altogether, as well as such controversial phrases as *vive la difference,* which would have been a terrible bore.

Instead, God paraded all the animals, two by two, in front of Adam until it dawned on him that there was a boy lion and a girl lion, a boy giraffe and a girl giraffe, and he began to put two and two together and said, "I seem to be missing somebody."

"By Jove, you've got it!" shouted God. "I thought you'd never notice . . . it is not good that man should be alone."

Then God got busy and set about putting together a special somebody just for Adam.

She would out-mane the lion, out-plume the peacock, and out-fox the fox. She would be so well put together that from then till Kingdom come, men would be apt to nudge one another, whistle, and gasp, "I say—is she well put together!"

Realizing that one earthy person was quite enough (and at times one too many), God decided that woman should not be made from the dust of the ground, but from a somewhat higher form of life. As Adam was the highest living form (being formed after the image and likeness of God himself), he was put to sleep with what was the first recorded use of anesthetic. Without so much as getting his signature on a medical release, God removed one of Adam's ribs and from it whittled Eve. She came complete with the designer label, "Adam's Rib." This turned her into a very designing woman.

Because of his dusty origins, man was predisposed to be a dusty person. To balance this, woman was programmed with an aversion to dust (and dirt and grime) that has had her shaking a duster in man's direction ever since . . . as well as asking him such things as, "Did you remember to wipe your feet before coming into the house?" and, "Are those your black finger marks all over the clean towels?"

In order that she would be the perfect complement to man, woman was built to fit. Where he stuck out, she didn't. Where she stuck out, he didn't. He had massive doses of testosterone, and she had massive doses of estrogen. He had hair on his face and chest, and she had a peaches and cream complexion, and a chest plus a chest.

Man had the ability to calculate figures, and woman had the figure worth calculating.

When all her checks and balances were made, God brought her to Adam.

He could have placed her in the middle of a petunia patch and had Adam stumble over her while walking through the garden. Or he could have had her kiss Adam awake in a reverse role-play of Sleeping Beauty. But he didn't.

God wanted to make it perfectly clear that he had specifically designed woman for man. He must have had exquisite pleasure in anticipating the gleam in Adam's eye when first he saw Eve. That glorious moment when all of creation sang, "Who giveth this woman to be united with this man?" and God, as both Father of the bride and Father of the groom (which, under normal circumstances, would have been recorded as a conflict of interest), said, "I do!"

What artist would dare to capture the mystery of that first long, lingering look! No awkward shyness, no posturing, no intimidation, no self-doubt, no fear of rejection . . . but the radiance of the perfection of man and woman mirrored in each other.

That moment holds eternity enthralled.

Details dazzle the imagination. Did they start from the bottom and look up, or did they start from the top and look down? Did Adam reach out to first stroke her hair, or did he first touch her lips in wonder? Did Eve take his hand in hers and hold it pressed against her heart?

They instigated life's supreme adventure. One

poet called it "the Divinest gift of fate ... to discover at a glance, the heart's true friend, the soul's true mate!"

The honeymoon was never meant to be over.

Adam was kicking up the dust somewhere, probably in a preliminary trial run to inventing the wheel, and Eve was polishing the fruit on the various trees in the garden, making effective use of her duster even then.

The apples on the tree of knowledge of good and evil looked as though they could use some polishing. Sitting under the branches was a gorgeous creature. As he saw Eve approach, he rose and bowed.

"EveN," he hissed, "How beguiling to see you here! In the name of liberté, fraternité, and equalité ... come sit, and talk a while."

Adam had never told her, "Don't sit under the apple tree with anyone else but me." At best he was a terrible communicator whose vocabulary was heavily weighted with, "Yup," "Nope," and "Uh-huh," so she supposed it would be all right. (As it turned out, it was all wrong.)

"Have an apple?" offered the serpent.

"Thanks, but no thanks," declined Eve.

She was trying to remember her Sunday School verse for the week. In the divine chain of command, God had taught it to Adam, and Adam had taught it to her (but not well enough): "Of every tree of the garden thou mayest freely eat; but of the tree of the knowledge of good and evil, thou shalt not eat of it; for in the day that thou eatest thereof thou shalt surely die" (Genesis 2:16–18).

"What is 'die'?" she had asked Adam.

"How should I know?" Adam replied with his customary insight. "God said it, we believe it, and that settles it!"

He made a mental note that as an extra precaution, he really should put a fence of barbed wire around the tree, with a flashing neon light to warn, "Trespassers will be prosecuted."

"Next Saturday morning, for sure," he thought, setting a trend of procrastination that man has lived to regret ever since.

"Did you know that an apple a day keeps the doctor away?" hissed the serpent.

"It's not on my diet," said Eve.

"Only 80 calories . . ."

"But the Surgeon General says that eating apples may be dangerous to our health."

"Balderdash!" hissed the serpent. "It's all hearsay! Test the facts for yourself. Try it, you might like it. Besides, can't you make even one solitary decision on your own? Haven't you ever thought of being EveN?"

Eve's eyes lit up!

"If you eat this fruit," continued the serpent, "you won't die—why, you will know the difference between good and evil and that will make you equal with God himself. You will be the founding mother of the equal rights movement—think of what that will mean to the National Organization for *Wo-men*."

"Hum-m-m," said Eve, picking a large red apple and crunching into it. "When you put it that way—it might be fun to know the difference between good and evil, and to make my mark in history, and I especially like the sound of EveN!"

"Eve . . ." called Adam.

"EveN," she corrected him immediately, surprised at the domineering snap to her voice. Feeling a new authority, she handed him the apple with the terse comment, "Eat!"

Adam paused a moment and thought, "This woman has been deceived, but I am not being deceived. I am doing this with my eyes open, not beguiled, in full command of all my faculties, with all clarity, come what may, so help me God" (1 Timothy 2:14).

"Delicious," he said as he munched it all the way down to the core.

"Adam, I don't have a thing to wear," whined EveN.

"So I've noticed," snickered Adam, handing her a bunch of fig leaves as he hid behind a bush.

"Now look what you've gone and done!" boomed the voice of God.

The lion started snarling at the lamb, and thorns and thistles sprung up from the ground.

"She made me do it," groaned Adam, pointing his finger at EveN, while beads of sweat formed on his brow.

"He made me do it," sobbed EveN, pointing her

finger at the serpent, and she noticed that she had a headache.

"The buck stops here," hissed the serpent, "but hiss-ss-tory will set the record straight," and he pointed the tip of his tail back to Adam and slithered off.

At Odds with EveN

> Blessed art thou, O Lord our God,
> King of the Universe,
> who has not made me
> a heathen,
> a bondman,
> a *woman.*

The jaundiced eye of the patriarchial society that grew like a thorn out of Eden was epitomized in this old Jewish prayer. It set Adam on a collision course with EveN.

The shining glory that was her role as complement to man corroded. Through the centuries, all that she was meant to be became instead all that man would let her be.

The gospel of Jesus Christ became her liberating force.

Moving out from under the stigma she carried as Eve of the forbidden fruit of Eden, she was anointed as Mary of the blessed fruit of Advent. Divinity affirmed her in his grace, cast himself dependent on her care, stooped to grow himself within her—then suckled at her breast.

From that point on, women forever more could

sing with Mary her hymn of restoration and praise:

"My soul doth magnify the Lord, and my spirit hath rejoiced in God my Saviour. For he hath regarded the low estate of his handmaiden; for, behold from henceforth all generations shall call me blessed . . ." (Luke 1:46–48).

What love but that of woman would demonstrate itself by the extravagance of costly perfume poured over the feet of the one she held beloved—then drying them with her hair!

After the crucifixion, the power of that same love stretched far beyond the constraints of logic. Before daybreak, notwithstanding the formidable security of armed guards on duty, and a heavy stone sealing the entrance to the tomb, Mary Magdalene (together with other women) took unguents with which to once again anoint the body of Jesus—this time in death.

This was the complement of a love that did not cower frightened, hidden in a room, but moved forward, determined to breach the barriers of separation from one beloved.

Heart-tearing astonishment and a flood of tears at seeing the empty tomb was but a prelude to the indescribable joy of the resurrection.

"Woman, why weepest thou?"

"Because they have taken away my Lord and I know not where they have laid him."

"Mary . . . " the simple endearment of her name.

"Rabboni!" soaring recognition.

Returning the compliment of her love, Jesus spoke the name "woman" as his *first* word of resurrection—he showed himself *first* to her—and he gave her the commission to be the *first* evangel, the bearer of the good news of his victory over death.

The men could not believe it!

As the women ran in, hearts bursting with excitement and jubilation, they were met with a wall of skepticism: "... Their words seemed to them [the disciples] as idle tales and they believed them not" (Luke 24:11).

They had to believe it! They saw for themselves—the sepulcher was empty, the linen burial cloths folded. They shouted with the women, "Hallelujah, Jesus Christ is risen indeed!"

At the turn of the century, scaffolds were scattered throughout the Chinese countryside. They hung like gallows against the tranquil landscape of rolling hills and paddies brilliant green with sprouting rice. These were "baby towers," monuments of death where step by laddered step women could climb to throw down their unwanted baby girls.

The Chinese people have, as one of their culture's prime characteristics, a love of children. But for the poorest of the poor, when there was yet another mouth to feed and not enough food, the boy took preference over the girl.

So gutted by oppression and superstition was the image of women in the old Chinese culture that baby boys were frequently dressed as little girls, complete with earrings and ribbons in their hair. This was to deceive the evil spirits, who would not bother to attack a girl.

The feet of little girls were cruelly bound with tapes that pulled the ball at one end of the arch towards the heel at the other. This was tightened regularly, and the so-called beauty of the "tiny feet" of the women of China was laid on a foundation of pain and grotesque deformity.

The liberating love of Jesus Christ sent missionaries to China. They unbound the feet of the women, and rescued the abandoned babies.

All around the world, the Christian gospel has delivered women from tribal rituals and atrocities that had led many of them to suicide as the only acceptable alternative.

Jesus Christ replaced oppression and despair with the promise of an equality of salvation and an equal inheritance of the Kingdom of God, regardless of sex, age, ethnic origin, or avowed political party!

In Christ there is no East or West, and there is neither male nor female (Galatians 3:28) but we are all one in the spirit.

Fortunately, we are not all one in the body.

Celebrating our equality as men and women in Christ does not preclude celebrating our differences as men and women. Therein lies the rub in the perils of the Pauline Epistles.

Plowing through all the interpretations, misinterpretations, appropriations, inappropriations, designations, connotations, quotes, and misquotes of the Apostle Paul is enough to grow hair on the chest of the most feminine of women!

It is indeed a puzzlement.

If the patriarchal society was bad, the matriarchal society may be worse.

In the book *The Coming Matriarchy*, co-authored with Laura Ashcraft, Elizabeth Nickles writes, "Women are changing in ways that will collide with and forever alter the comfortable contours of our social and economic topography. They are assuming characteristics associated with leadership—becoming more aggressive, independent, authoritative, decisive and goal-oriented."

With many seminaries reporting that between 30 and 40 percent of students enrolled are now women, the comfortable contours of our theological topography may also be forever altered.

Walking across the high-tension wire of controversy, we take the balance pole that has at one end the chauvinistic parody of Paul shouting, "Put a woman in to preach? They're an emotional sort—they'll speak up for women's choices with their shrill and squeaky voices, if we ever put a woman in to preach!" (1 Corinthians 14:34–35).

At the other end, liturgical feminism pushes its demands for a sexual textual revolution throughout the scriptures. A "she for a he," and a "he for a she," that castrates out of the book of Psalms alone more than two hundred pronouns, neuters the Fatherhood of God to a suggested "Heavenly Parent," "Eternal One," or "Divine Providence," and androgynizes the *son*ship of Christ to a male/female inclusive as "child" of God. We teeter on the edge of Matthew, Mark, Luke, and Joan, and the possibility of a God and Goddess translation of the Bible that raises as its flag Galatians 3:28.

The one end spells sudden death to the ordination of women, and the other to the credibility of biblical feminism.

Somewhere in the middle is the right place to grip, but where?

Being a rather tolerant sort, anxious to understand alternative points of view, I read *Let Me Be a Woman,* by Elizabeth Eliot, and *I Am a Woman by God's Design,* by Beverly LaHaye, and I say "You're absolutely right!"

Then I read *Our Struggle to Serve,* by Virginia Hearn, and *The Apostle Paul and Women in the Church,* by Don Williams, and I say, "You're absolutely right!"

Then the party of the first part says to the party of the second part that I must be a dolt to agree with such diverse attitudes, and I say, "You're absolutely right!"

It all boils down to the fact that there is a little bit of good in the worst of what has been written, and a little bit of bad in the best of what has been written, and it makes me shudder to think of what next might be written.

I am somewhat abashed to say that my own personal struggle has not been so much to serve, but more frequently to find some loophole out through which I could wiggle my way not to serve!

Having a disposition that enjoys "elevenses," and four o'clock with crumpets and hot tea, as well as flower arranging, classical ballet, and lolling on my backside watching the clouds go by, whenever I am asked if I could serve, I am inclined to blanch and ask the person doing the asking if they really think I am the one that should; and then God reminds me that I told him that I would ... however, whenever, wherever and in whatever way he may choose, come what may. I remember that I started my day that morning, with the first open wink of an eye, as I do every morning—by emptying myself of myself and asking the Holy Spirit to fill me to overflowing, and to live his life through mine.

Suddenly, the applicable opportunity of my commitment whomps me. I say, "Oh, bother!" and leave my flowers, and my tea, and the glorious music of "Les Sylphides," and go to my knees with the resolution that I should if I could ... so I would.

As a result of a commitment to obedience that prays never to quench the flow of the Holy Spirit through my life, and asks forgiveness for being perverse in wanting to do only that which I want to do, rather than that which the Lord wants me to do, I have ended up serving where a lot of people, myself included, would prefer not to serve ... such as in the horrid research necessary to stand against the degeneracy of pornography.

It is one thing to serve in the glorious experience of sharing the speaker's platform at Christian women's retreats and conferences, where the joy of the Lord flows to strengthen the ties that bind us first to him, then to each other.

It is another to serve in the traumatizing experience of entering the cross-cultures that are the tap roots of moral erosion. Yet, where more necessary to shine the light of the redemptive love of Jesus Christ?

As I tearfully struggled to find an excuse by which I could avoid serving in that arena, I prayed, "Lord, here am I—please send someone else," and I very efficiently rattled off some half-dozen names of spiritual giants in the faith who would be highly qualified as having the intestinal fortitude with which to cope with human depravity.

The Lord replied, "But Fay—YOU are my someone else."

Without compromising my commitment, what could I say but a shaky, "Yes."

Taking Philippians 4:8, "Finally brethren, whatsoever things are true, whatsoever things are honest, whatsoever things are just—pure—lovely—of *GOOD REPORT*, think on these things," as the windshield wiper to cleanse my mind (moment by moment) of the filth being put into it; and strengthened by my pastor, who stood by my side and prayerfully pledged his full support, I went out to slay the giants of organized crime.

In my struggle not to serve, I found heartache that had no ease as I entered the world of the sexually abused child. Suddenly I saw Jesus weeping over Jerusalem, only Jerusalem was Los Angeles, San Francisco, Chicago, New York, Dallas, and the trickle down to the little towns of America where depravity

tries to hide as it twists and misuses the lives of
these his little ones.

I discovered that a day in the life of an ordinary
housewife may include picketing a porno store; a radio or television interview; debating the explosive
and anguished homosexual issue on many college
platforms; being called a "fundamental fascist" and
seeing your name written up with those of your colleagues in a hard-core magazine opposite the picture
of a naked bride with flowers in her groin.

In my struggle not to serve, I found my equilibri-
um balanced by Wedgwood china, Waterford crystal,
and East Indian curry served piping hot with exotic
condiments on a rotating tray. I found friends who
did not shunt me off as a social hazard, or try to
change the conversation when someone asked what I
had been doing lately, but who said, "Decorum be
damned—tell it as it is!" and cared enough to join
their breaking hearts with mine as our tears dripped
over the cherries flambé.

I learned that although the doors of opportunity
that the Lord opens for us are not always the doors
of our preference, the faithfulness in our call to obedience, "come what may," taps the grace of God's
strength as our all sufficiency.

I also learned that by being willing to stick my
neck out, I ended up seeing a lot more of the world!

In confronting the serious moral and ethical questions of reproductive manipulation—the holocaust of
abortion, wombs for rent, gender selection, among
many others, I entered the fascinating science of ge-
netics.

Instead of spending endless hours caught up in the coffee klatch, I spent endless hours in research libraries and listening to lectures by some of the nation's top scientists, assimilating data on all the awesome possibilities and ramifications of the recreation of life.

By breaking out of the comfortable cloister of merely watering my own spiritual rose garden, I learned that the expanded dimensions of the Christian witness are exciting, exhilarating, at times very entertaining, and exhausting!

In celebrating our differences as men and women, somewhere in time the domestic woman has been sold down the river as an addle-headed nitwit.

She is anything but!

Conscious of her alternatives and vulnerable to the contrast of accolades poured on women of achievement in education, finance, and the arts, she winces at this sociological squint.

The diversity of her role as a generalist, maneuvering the multitransitions of her own life, as well as those in her family, coupled with the opportunities of her community involvement, make hers one of the most demanding of all careers.

In a long overdue tribute, the *Wall Street Journal* published an ad from United Technologies Corporation of Hartford, Connecticut:

THE MOST CREATIVE JOB IN THE WORLD ...

It involves taste, fashion, decorating, recreation, education, transportation, psychology, romance, cuisine, designing, literature, medicine, handicraft, art, horticulture, economics, government, community relations, pediatrics, entertainment, maintenance, purchasing, direct mail, law, accounting, religion, energy and management.

Anyone who can handle all those has to be somebody special. She is. She's a homemaker!

A positive from all the negatives in the demise of the dollar, and high interest rates that make negotiating a home mortgage comparable to the most complicated of corporate wheeling and dealing, is that owning a *house* has now become an apex of achievement. Concurrently, the traditional woman, pivoting as housewife in that house, is worth her weight in gold. When I scrub my kitchen walls and floor, I consider in awe, "Aye, now—there alone is $10,000 of spit and polish gleaming!" I chalk up my doctorate in domesticity which, in today's economy, is worth probably considerably more than a Ford Foundation Grant to keep bugs jumping under a microscope!

Reinforcing the worth of the woman in the home is a first step to removing her from the endangered species list, and a primary requirement in stabilizing the shaking foundations of the family, the backbone of the country and the church.

With all the hullabaloo over the ordination of women, there is a tendency to elevate the pulpit above the pew.

Pity.

I find the pew diverse, flexible, and far more liberating. No power play with the board of deacons; no reassignment on the Bishop's whim to the Archdiocese of Antarctica; no passing the plate for a pay raise; and, instead of Hebrew, Greek, and homiletics, the Sunday funnies and several long, slow cups of coffee before ambling down to church!

When I read of the anger of a woman who said that when she was served communion by twenty-five "males" and no "females," she reached a point of resentment where she felt she could not even take communion, I was crushed by sadness—to see, much less count, twenty-five "males" instead of Christ!

I am usually passed communion by the person sitting next to me in the pew. In some churches, the message is whispered from one to the other, "This do in remembrance of Me." Sometimes it is a little child who carefully tries to steady the tray with its tiny wobbling cups of wine. Sometimes it is my own dear daughter, or son, or husband, or favorite friend. Sometimes it is age, whose vein-lined shaking hand I want to kiss as I take the broken bread.

I think the spirit of the love of Christ would be enhanced if, during the communion service, we would deliberately choose to sit next to someone who had irritated us, or hurt us, or annoyed us, so that in the sharing of the cup we may be cleansed by enacting the words of the Carmelite priest St. John of the Cross, "Where there is no love, put love and you will find love. . . ."

Not frequently, but at very special times, we share communion here at home—with new friends or old friends, or maybe just ourselves. Then each one present has the joy of saying a special word of remembrance of him as we serve one another.

As *kamikaze* pilots shouted, "Tora! Tora! Tora!" and struck at Pearl Harbor, the guns of war sailed down the Whangpoo River into the Chinese port of Shanghai. Together with 600 others, my mother and I were taken as POWs and shipped up the Grand Canal made famous by Marco Polo, to a camp at Yangchow. Perhaps the most significant communion services in my memory were those we shared there during our 2½ years of internment.

This was the most leveling experience of my life; the common denominator of starvation and suffering is the most equalizing factor in the human condition.

Woman has stood as a very necessary complement to man through the bloodbath of many wars. She loaded muskets and fought by his side with the Minutemen; as a nurse she died in foreign fields where her cross, too, marks a place, row on row. She drove ambulances in the Battle of Britain, and shared the equal right of torture and death in the gas chambers of Auschwitz.

Rosie the Riveter kept the assembly lines rolling and, best of all, the home fires burning.

Lest we forget, women also served who only stood to wait . . . all too often their hands clutching little fingers as caskets were unloaded. The brightly folded flag her recompense, the waiting woman held it tightly to her heart and drew from its strength courage in the darkness of the lonely night—she carried on alone and grew the family through those war-filled years.

In the shabbiest of circumstances in that prison camp, man and woman rose to new heights of dignity in their complement one to the other. Roots of beauty were dug in the simplicity of caring and sharing exchanged in the common cause—survival. It was not unusual to see a woman break in half the ration of her slice of bread and share it with a man whose larger frame hung the more gaunt from hunger. He in turn would see that her pail was filled with water from the well, a woman's aching arms-distance away.

There, too, we shared communion. We saved our rationed bread to break and pass. We had no wine, but just as sweet was the pale tea, diluted, almost colorless. We were a shabby, raggy crew, suddenly gowned in glory by his grace, as we remembered... the washing of the feet, the crown of thorns, the scourge, the cross and spear-pierced side.

Remembrance of the Easter dawn, the empty tomb, and the power of the resurrected life transfused us with new courage. We could look to the guards marching atop the walls that imprisoned us, and say with Paul, "Neither death nor life, neither messenger of Heaven nor monarch of earth, neither what happens today nor what may happen tomorrow, neither a power from high nor a power from below, nor anything else in God's whole world has any power to separate us from the love of God in Christ Jesus our Lord!" (Romans 8:38, Phillips translation).

I take communion as a lover's moment, secluded with my Lord.

At that time I pray no intercessory prayer—I shut out the world and the people around me so that I may better remember *only him*. It is an act of love and worship that I would seek to orchestrate only by the throbbing of my prostrate heart....

Father, I adore you, lay my life before you, how I

love you! Jesus, I adore you. . . . Spirit, I adore you. . . .

Twenty-five men could not serve me communion, nor could twenty-five women, not even twenty-five angels. Only Christ can serve me communion!

It was thrilling to me, as a Christian woman, when Mother Teresa won the Nobel Peace Prize.

It is spiritually significant to note that it was not awarded to the Pope, or to Dr. Billy Graham, or to Dr. Anybody Else, but to a simple serving *woman,* who went where others did not want to go.

As a complement to all mankind, she holds both men and women, dying in her arms; she serves—the cup of cold water in his name, and lets the love of Jesus flow through the channel of her life.

She wears a *woman's veil,* as bride of Christ. She has no pulpit, nor parish, but she has spoken in pulpits and parishes around the world. Her prayer of equal rights?

> Dear Jesus—help me to spread thy fragrance everywhere I go. Flood my soul with thy Spirit and life. Penetrate and possess my whole being so utterly that all my life may only be a radiance of thine. Shine through me and be so in me that every soul I come in contact with may feel thy presence. Let them look up and see no longer me, but only Christ. . . . Let me preach thee without preaching. Not by words, but by my example. By the catching force, the sympathetic influence of what I do—the evident fullness of the love my heart bears to thee. . . ."

The cartoonist CONRAD paid her tribute in the *Los Angeles Times* with a simple line drawing of her weathered face, and a caption that is more eloquent than volumes of words: *"Why be a priest when you can be a saint!"*

Science, building a bridge over the troubled waters of biological destiny, is at last on the threshold of solving the feminine mystique and the gusto behind the macho man.

There is a difference between the male and female brain. Testosterone, which develops the male genitalia, also masculinizes brain tissue; estrogen, produced by the female ovaries, feminizes brain tissue.

Writing for *Discover* magazine in April 1981, Pamela Weintraub says, "Yes, male and female brains do differ." She goes on to affirm that "behavioral and intellectual differences between the sexes are partly rooted in the structure of the brain." That women are inherently superior in some areas of endeavor, and men in others, is a fact that she maintains "would in no way undermine legitimate demands for social equality," but would result in a better understanding between the sexes.

Dr. Eleanor Maccoby of Stanford stresses the enormous "overlap" of male/female characteristics, yet she states that boys have certain things going for them, and girls have certain things going for them— the differences complement and compensate for each other, and it is "fortunate that we're both together in the same world co-operating!"

It is in that cooperation that we find the essence of our complement, one to the other.

During my elementary school days, we used to tease each other with the ditty, "Adam and Eve and Pinch-Me went down to the river to swim. Adam and

Eve jumped in—who do you think was left?"

After several doses of "Pinch-Me's," both on the receiving and the giving end, I decided to change the wording to, "Adam and Eve and Hug-Me-Tight went down to the river to swim. . . ."

Early, I discovered that it was far more complimentary and comfortable to be hugged than to be pinched, and the popularity of the tease then increased not only among the student body, but among the teachers as well.

God gave us arms to wrap around each other.

In the intoxicating lure of the arts, the one that epitomizes our tandem role as man and woman is the showcase of the *grand pas de deux* in classical ballet.

During my studio years, I learned the necessity of strong, sensitive partnering. The slightest touch can hold a balance, missed timing can wreak disaster.

At a dress rehearsal of the "Aurora's Wedding" *pas de deux* from the ballet *Sleeping Beauty*, I ran across the stage, rose *en pointe* to take a *penche* (bending) arabesque against the hands of my kneeling partner, and . . . he was not there! He had paused, for the fraction of a moment, to adjust a shoe—he missed a beat, and I fell flat on my face. Of course in performance he would have let the shoe fall off rather than miss a beat, but the flaw became a touchstone of remembrance between us.

The exquisite line of the ballerina that flows from her fingertips through the lyrical curve of her leg, to reach for infinity in the stretch of arch and pointed toe, is held aloft in breathless wonder as woman places her confidence in the strength of man. He holds her with the illusion that if he were to let go she would fly out of his grasp. He has timed her every turn, or leap. He is there to balance her, to steady her, and to catch her.

He is the enabler and enhancer of her grace. He pulls from her impossibilities of interpretation and technique. He revels in the fragile glory of her form, yet knows the ramrod of her endurance and her strength.

As they perform their individual solo divertissement, the ballerina feathers her steps across the stage with ethereal lightness. She spins in pirouettes and holds, seemingly forever, the line that reaches up to heaven. She is Eve—enchanting and elusive.

The *danceur* fairly boils up from the wings with a series of *grande jete* leaps that brings out bursts of applause. His vigor, elevation, and power defy gravity. He crouches and pounces to beat his legs against a quickening tempo set to match his muscle. He is Adam, subduing the earth.

In the grande finale, they dance together to celebrate the perfect harmony of their love—one has a glimpse of Paradise revisited.

As they bow in curtain calls, he presents her proudly to the audience, then offers a bouquet, from which she takes a rose, kisses it, and gives it back to him.

She is EveN—God's complement to man.

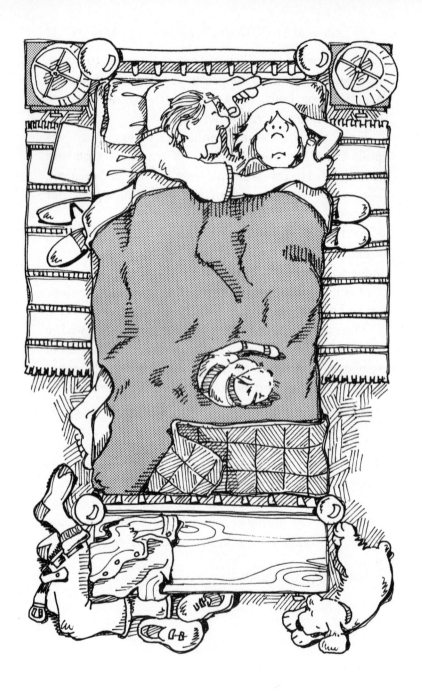

For Good, Better, & Best—
Marriage, That Is!

The weight of John's arm was crushing my ribs, and his rhythmic breathing was blowing hot air all over my face—it was like sleeping with a blast furnace.

"Romance befuddled," I thought. "There are times when it is downright uncomfortable!"

I had been awake for over an hour, jolted by a subliminal alert that stems from the core of restless thought.

Now when you are wide awake in the middle of the night, thinking, and the person next to you is sound asleep, that person frequently becomes the focus of your thinking. The fact that he is sound asleep, and you are wide awake when you would prefer to be sound asleep, colors your waking thoughts towards him—and many cases of slander have gone through the docket to prove the point.

As an out-and-out romanticist, I have always felt that life should be orchestrated with a sound track comparable to that of a Cecil B. deMille extravaganza; and that love should have as its prelude a rapture like that caught by the promoters of Tabu perfume. Their ad, enduring through the years and hidden in the fantasies of generations of women, shows a pause in the melody as a tuxedo-clad violinist clutches his startled pianist in unrestrained desire. His arm embraces her wasplike waist, and the gossamer of her skirt billows provocatively over the piano bench. We never do see her face, but his is the chiseled answer to a maiden's prayer.

Projecting myself into the ad, I imagine a continuum of desperate courtship to the marriage bed, the passionate climax of which would rise with a crescendo of strings playing, "Ah, Sweet Mystery of Life, at Last I've Found You!" The morning after would be kissed into awareness with breathless moans of lyrical ecstasy, followed by a breakfast of peaches and cream served on a rose-bedecked tray. Languid and alluring, all I would ever have to worry about is buying satin sheets, and the regular use of Oil of Olay for a silken skin he would yearn to touch.

As it was, the luminous dial on the digital clock in our bedroom spun over to 3:57 A.M. The night sounds of my wedded bliss were the steady drip of a faucet that had needed a new washer for several months and the guttural wheezes that came from my husband's grotesquely contorted face as he struggled to breathe through one nostril. The other was smothered against bunches of blue forget-me-nots printed on the pillow case.

I sat up and stared at him.

Heart of my heart, light of my eyes, and the total

resource of any romantic image I might try to conjure up in our marriage; after twenty-five years I was buffeted between the double tension of knowing him too well, and wondering whether I really knew him at all.

A far cry from the violin strings of Brahms, Beethoven, and Bach, his music was Benny Goodman through the Swinging Years. Instead of chiseled poetry, his rugged features were strictly High Noon at the O.K. Corral.

We did have gossamer—once. On our honeymoon, four layers of beribboned nylon, in the best of my trousseau white, tangled round about us. Far from languid and alluring, I giggled hysterically, and he cursed, "Where does the bloody stuff end!"

There were no morning-after peaches and cream, but there were runs hand-in-hand along the shore, and mystery walks through pine-scented forest paths. There was a touch of morning madness when, caught within the spell of pungent earth and blackberries, ripe along a mossy bank, we shed our clothes and frolicked in the seclusion of a mountain stream. The bed stones were slippery and the current bumped bruises on our bottoms, through waters cold as ice. We dressed slowly, in the warmth of a sunbeam, intoxicated by what we called our Eden adventure.

In British tradition, I had preceded my bridesmaids down the aisle, and our vows came out of the Episcopal Book of Common Prayer. "The Form of Solemnization of Matrimony," from good King

James' Royal Days, with thee's and thou's and here-tofores . . .

John stirred.

"Are you awake? I asked.

"No," he sniffed.

"Wake up," I nudged. "I've been lying here thinking . . ."

"Careful," he interrupted. "It might become a habit!"

"Seriously," I said. "I've been thinking over our marriage vows. Give me a ten-point outline of your 'worse.'"

"My what?"

"Your 'worse.' You know—the love and the cherish, the in sickness and in health, the for richer or for poorer. I've been thinking about the for better or for worse and it's the 'worse' that's got me worried! I need to know exactly what I took you for, until death us do part."

"Good heavens," he yawned, "couldn't it wait 'till morning?"

Then he chuckled, winked, and pulled me down to snuggle on his chest.

"Forget the 'worse,' honey. I'll never get tired of holding your hand. You and I are going to make it for good, better, and best!"

Three words, uttered in the middle of the night, caught an ultimate in the directional for marriage as it's meant to be.

The richer or poorer is circumstantial, the sickness and health is providential, the better is alluring, but plighting one's troth to a "worse" is nothing less than reinforcing bad behavior. It is giving witness before all the dearly beloved gathered together that we can be as rotten as we like to each other and we will still stick it through.

With all the criminal elements worsening up the world, who needs it at the altar? It is the worse, worser, and worst in each of us that is filling our divorce courts.

Someone once said that if marriage is the seventh sacrament, divorce might now be considered the eighth.

Half the people I know are not married and wish that they were; 80 percent of the other half are married and wish that they weren't. One constant that does not change is the agonizing hurt of shattered relationships.

As devastating as it is, loneliness without a partner may not be as abrasive as loneliness with a partner who does not understand, who does not communicate, and who long since stopped caring.

By temperament, the average man checks out as a cross between Winnie-the-Pooh and Hitler. He is either full of honey and cozies up with the warm fuzzies, or he is a violent explosion that sets the home fires blazing—frequently out of control.

The average woman fluctuates on a slightly broader base (especially when she sits down). She is Little Mary Sunshine, and the glad game of Pollyanna; the manipulative tactics of Mata Hari; or the broom-riding finesse of the Wicked Witch from the West.

Given these factors, we mull them together and come up with a love quotient that thrusts us into what Peter Marshall called the Halls of Highest Human Happiness.

We are an imperfect people, looking for the perfect partner with whom to live out our perfect romantic dream. The static of our diversities interrupt that dream and we find ourselves with the lights turned off, alone in the dark.

Hearts ice up in a resistance to intimacy, and freeze-frame in a holding pattern of "worse."

There are marriages that never should have been. They are mutations bred of human error, and God forgives us.

But most are born in crested love and spirits full of hope. Yet they, too, teeter through the years, held in fragile balance of all that is good, or "worse," in man and wife.

We *can* move up from sliding scales of "worse." There is a *good,* there is an even *better,* and always, there is the ultimate *best!*

We lost a towering oak during last winter's rains. It stood and canopied our home. It nested jays and caught a kite entangled in its heights. It brushed the stars at night and shimmered in the eerie light of many crescent moons. It weathered lightning, thunder, and the frequent tremors of California's quaking earth. Pruned by the fury of a Santa Ana wind, it snapped its branches and warmed our hearth with slow, long burning logs.

I loved that oak.

It fell. We counted rings and aged it at three hundred years or more. Having stood fast through centuries of stormy onslaught, it died, eroded at the root by tiny borer bugs and rot that hollowed out its strength.

Those little things that grate, and chafe, and dig, and pick, and nag.

Love seldom dies. It tarnishes and, lacking luster, dulls and sometimes simply fades away.

Little things help keep it shining bright. Small acts of kindness warm and joy our hearts; gentle words stroke fears and say, "*I* believe in *you!*" Bits of fun break the tension of a stress.

As I race around the country speaking at various conferences, getting ready to bed down for the night is often a lonely time. What a comfort it is to open up my suitcase and find a note from my husband pinned to my nightie, that says "Wish I were here!"

During one midwinter freeze, my son threw a pair of his red and white striped long-johns into my case, and said, "Here Mom, it's cold in Minneapolis, you'd better sleep in these." When I went to pull them on that night, my husband's note read, "Thank God, I'm not!"

Nothing is so small as to be insignificant. Jesus numbers each hair on our heads.

Ruskin said, "In mortals there is a care for trifles which proceeds from love and conscience, and is most holy; and a care for trifles which comes of idleness and frivolity, and is most base."

The wisdom lies in sifting through the difference.

During a radio interview with Dr. James Dobson, I teased him about his book *What Wives Wished Their Husbands Knew About Women.*

"My disposition," I said, "bends towards what wives thank God their husbands *don't know* about women, and pray they never find out!"

He threw back his head and howled.

Some things we confront head on, others we can walk around. By our response, or lack of it, we set the limit beyond which we will not go without direct, and sometimes painful, confrontation. We program attitudes towards ourselves and inherit the behavioral patterns we have reinforced.

I heard one woman hiss, *"Love* is just another four letter word."

She had been subjected to eight years of verbal battering and physical abuse. At last she went for help. Through therapy the bullying tactics stopped and mutual changepoints were established. Her marriage is not yet good, but she has moved it out of "worse."

The patterns of our live-and-let-live are cut in mutual tolerance; a perspective that sees first the beam in our own eye, before the splinter in another.

My own glaring flaws humble me to tolerant reciprocity, like the girl who listed endless qualities she would demand in any man she married, and then was asked, "And what have you to offer in return?"

There are facets of my nature I try to hide from everyone, my husband most of all. He does not need to know the many times I smoulder with resentment and would like to konk him over the head with the proverbial rolling pin. It is called restraint and biting my tongue, lest I blurt out barbs that prick and hurt and find myself impaled on petty trifles.

A Chinese philosopher urged, "Think three times before you speak." Confucius said, "Twice is enough."

Mary "pondered all these things within her heart" (Luke 2:19); she quietly thought things through.

I used to rant and rave a lot. I majored in the minors.

I have a tendency to think that there is only one way to do anything, and it is my way. I like quick efficiency and lose patience with those who just plod through a task, especially if it is a task concerning me. This gives me a disposition to steamroller through and take over.

After one appalling family confrontation that involved not only my husband, son, and daughter, but had me cracking the whip even at the cat and dog, my husband snarled, "You remind me of the woman on the can of Old Dutch cleanser—rushing around, waving a big stick, stirring up even the air around you!"

"Rubbish!" I reacted. "I'm getting things done! You remind me of a butt-inski, cranky Old Goat!"

We stopped in our tracks, took stock, and burst out laughing.

The hurtful truth is, he was right. I frequently am that Old Dutch cleanser woman, charging around with my apron flying. I have had to pause, and ask God to develop in me the "ornament of a meek and quiet spirit, which is in the sight of God, great price" (1 Peter 3:4). This modifies my bombastic nature and gives the rest of the family a chance to function on their own level without my bossy interference.

Now when we rub each other the wrong way, all John and I have to say is, *"O.D."* (Old Dutch) or *"O.G."* (Old Goat) and we both shift gears.

Or—instead of ranting and raving over petty trifles, when I get irritated with some of his peculiarities (and he is the first to deny he has any), I just work out my frustrations by scrubbing down the grout in the shower stall . . . with his toothbrush! (One of the things I thank God my husband does not know, and I pray he never finds out!) The spin-off is that I feel vindicated, we have a spotless shower, and he sports a bright Old Dutch smile.

Ruth Graham was asked if she had ever thought of divorcing Billy. She hesitated a moment, then said, "Divorce? No. Murder—yes!" Hopefully, Billy does not know.

Miss Piggy has it right. "Can a woman ever really know what is in the heart of a man?" she asks. "No, never—she can only guess. That is life. The good news is, men can only guess what is in the heart of a woman. And they are lousy guessers."

I opt to keep 'em guessing.

Paul says, "Esteem each other more highly than yourselves" (Philippians 2:3). This is the keynote of respect that stretches the dimensions of our love with the heart attitude, "You are more important to me, than me—your happiness is more important to me, than mine."

In developing a comfortable intimacy, we so frequently tend to put everything but each other first.

Pity.

It is dazzling to be first in someone's life, whether we are the ones doing the putting, or we are the ones being put. Preferably both.

Looking beyond all that we are not, and moving all that we are under the potential of all that we can become together in Christ: that is the encouraging, the enabling, and the ennobling of our commitment.

As television cameras around the world beamed the splendor and pageantry of the royal wedding into millions of homes, what an inspiration it was to hear the Archbishop of Canterbury give Prince Charles and Lady Diana the undergirding of spiritual commitment and direction:

> To know God more clearly.
> To follow him more nearly.
> To love him more dearly.

My husband and I chose to have engraved within our wedding rings a line from William Carey: "One for the other, and both for God."

After the assassination attempt on the life of the President, Nancy Reagan was interviewed by *Parade* magazine. "It's a particular kind of trauma that never leaves you once you've known it," she said. "It makes your times together so much more precious and your priorities are changed."

She went on to say that she did not think that

people worked at marriage as hard as they should. "It certainly isn't all 50-50. *Ever*. Sometimes it's 90-10. And you have to be willing to give the 90 percent. Or he to give the 90."

She struck a syncopated beat of mutual give and take.

She maintained that marriages often fail because the moment something goes wrong, one or the other partner gives up and says, "That's it! I'm leaving!" instead of communicating and trying to work things through.

She should know—she has "worked" her marriage through for thirty years.

In his book *Mortal Lessons,* Dr. Richard Selzer uses his pen to perform surgery on the human spirit as effectively as he uses his scalpel on the human body.

In order to remove a tumor from the cheek of a young woman, he had to cut a small facial nerve. It left her mouth twisted—"clownish," he said.

As he stood in the hospital room he watched the exchange between the young husband and wife.

"Who are they, I ask myself, he and this wry-mouth I have made, who gaze at and touch each other so generously, greedily?"

The young woman asks him if her mouth will always be twisted, and the surgeon has to tell her, "Yes, it will. It is because the nerve was cut."

"She nods and is silent," Selzer writes, "But the young man smiles. 'I like it,' he says, 'It is kind of cute.' All at once I *know* who he is. I understand, and

I lower my gaze. One is not bold in an encounter with a god. Unmindful, he bends to kiss her crooked mouth, and I so close I can see how he twists his own lips to accommodate to hers, to show her that their kiss still works. . . ."

Selzer lowers his gaze to "let the wonder in."

We bend, and twist ourselves to fit—that stirs in us divinity!

Some marriages need miracles. It is significant that Jesus performed his first miracle at a marriage. He has been performing miracles there ever since.

He worked a miracle for Margaret. Her marriage not only survived, but moved out of the safety zone of mediocrity and into the exciting potential that makes her every day a challenging new adventure of faith.

If anyone knew anything about women, it should have been Solomon. As kids we used to quip:

King David and King Solomon led very merry lives,
With many, many lady friends, and many, many wives.
When old age came upon them, with many, many qualms,
King Solomon wrote the Proverbs, and King David wrote the Psalms!

Yet Solomon tells us, "There be three things which are too wonderful for me, yea four which I know not: The way of an eagle in the air; the way of a serpent upon a rock; the way of a ship in the midst of the sea; and *the way of a man with a maid*" (Proverbs 30:18–19).

Centuries later, through countless volumes of analytical words, *the way of a man with a maid* is still too wonderful for us.

The awesome power of human sexuality that makes us one in the flesh so often is the force that drives us asunder. Statistics show approximately 62 percent of the couples seeking therapy do so because of sexual dissatisfaction. One therapist estimates that 85 percent of married couples "have failed to utilize their God-given sexual potential."

Most often the man feels that if their sex life were better, the marriage would be happier; and the woman feels that if their marriage were happier, their sex life would be better!

She feels that a comfortable intimacy should lead the way to sex, and he feels that sex is what leads the way to comfortable intimacy.

Margaret's marriage had fallen into frustrated confusion. Her miracle took a balance of divine intervention, a teachable spirit, and her own willingness to let the miracle begin in her.

In each of us, there is a bit of Margaret.

We sat on the edge of a bubbling hot jacuzzi, and took turns running our feet across the power jets. Bunches of tawny curls were caught at the nape of her neck and twisted through a tortoise shell comb. A few wisps straggled down her forehead and teased eyebrows tilted to accent a face arranged with piquant curiosity. Her lithe figure paid tribute to the disciplines of diet and exercise.

"She must have been stunning in her prime," I

thought, and bristled at the warp of time. It had set
her jaw in a grim contrast to gentle eyes, now brim-
ming with tears.

"There is no doubt," she said, "*I* drove him into
the arms of another woman."

It was an unusual admission. I gave her a quizzical
look.

"He was a silent lover. The only way he could
communicate his affection for me was through his
body. He never said a word—no endearments, no
verbal flirtations, just a fierce sexual appetite. It was
completely one-sided; I was never gratified. After a
few limp tries at talking things through, I quit. The
whole experience, which was never good, went down
the skids to bad, then on to progressive stages of
worse. I was frigid."

"Did you consider therapy?" I asked.

"Yes," she said, "but he wouldn't go. Even to sug-
gest it was an affront to his pride. But I went. I
didn't like what I was told . . . you know, the old story of relief through various techniques of self-gratifi-
cation. But one thing I did learn, and that was, if my
marriage needed help, and he was unwilling to seek
it, *I* was the only one able to do anything about it—
provided, of course, that I still cared enough to want
to try.

"I did care. That was the brutal hurt."

She paused and carefully dried each toe. I noticed
polish chipping off the nails, and brown age spots
dappling her hands.

"I decided to compromise. There was a lot that

was good in our marriage. We had three lovely kids, my husband was a decent father and a good provider, it was *just* our sex life that stank. That is the galling part. My *just* was his *most!* With that kind of a guy, I don't care how good a woman is in the kitchen, how trim, slim, or sleek an image she maintains, if she can't keep him happy in bed, she stands the risk of losing him."

"Yeah?" I countered, "But what about him keeping her happy in bed? Don't you think it's a two-way street?"

"In my case, no." She wagged a finger to emphasize the point. "I don't think I'm unique. I'll bet most women are satisfied to coast along in the warm security of the 'good-Buddy, I'll thank God for what I've got' partnership. I could have gone on, probably indefinitely, but he couldn't."

I thought of a friend whose husband had gone through the Battle of Britain. His body had been hit by shrapnel, and he was impotent. Yet they seemed to have an intimacy and love in their marriage that stretched beyond the sexual dimension.

Another woman wrote to Dear Abby that, despite the bungled operation which resulted in the loss of her husband's sexual desire, their love for each other did not lessen. "When we cuddle up in each other's arms on a cold winter night," she wrote, "we achieve a more lasting closeness than those couples who make love for three minutes, then leave each other to go to sleep in separate beds."

The ying and the yang of our options!

Margaret caught her husband in his office in the arms of his secretary—a girl young enough to be his daughter. In the two seconds it took her to open the door, her world blew away.

That night, she confronted him—to be faithful or not? He chose not. The irony was, he held her tenderly for most of the night. In the morning he packed and left.

The 4 Ds of marriage are depression, despair, drink, and divorce.

Margaret hit the bottle—heavily.

Her husband had walked out on her for another woman, so she felt that she had failed as a wife. Her friends were getting sick and tired of listening to her cries of loneliness, so she felt that she was failing even them. There was no light at the end of her tunnel; she could not see through the darkness, so she gave up.

Fortunately, God didn't.

One night, just as she was about to pour another vodka, the phone rang. It was a neighbor who had been trying for months to get her to a weekly Bible study. She was a sweet girl, but Margaret had written her off.

"She didn't come across with an intellectual snap," she said. "I figured she was just another do-gooder, mesmerized into the escape mechanism of religion. The fact that I was escaping through booze didn't enter my rationale."

Who calendars our hearts and marks the moment of our greatest need? At what particular point does heaven reach down and let the glory in? Angels, unaware, who intersect our lives, may live next door.

Margaret's voice broke, "She cared enough to drop everything and come right over. She perked some fresh coffee and, taking my hands in hers, with tears running down her face, she told me how much God loved me."

"It seemed so trite—but, God knows, I needed someone to tell me somebody loved me! I had nothing to lose. I no longer wanted my life, my husband no longer wanted my life, if God wanted it, He could have it."

That night Margaret stumbled through a prayer of desperation and laid the tattered remnants of her life in the hands of a Savior who said, simply, "Come . . . to me." Then she passed out on the living room sofa.

The next day she went to the Bible study. It became a weekly commitment.

"The word of God became my therapist," she said.

She spent hours pouring over the concordance in her Bible. She looked up every reference she could find to wives, husbands, and marriage. She could not do anything to change her husband's attitude, he was not even around. But she could search her own heart, and she did.

Through the women in her small discussion group, Margaret found support, encouragement, and intercessory prayer. They taught her to pray, and that she needed not only to look up for divine intervention, but that she needed to look down and seek out practical applications of the scriptures that could be used as change agents in her life.

"I cried out to God to do something . . . and he did, *in me!*" she said.

This was a dimension that she had not bargained for. It was a humiliating experience. She asked God to pinpoint her faults—the areas where she was responsible for creating many of her own problems, not only with her husband, but in the totality of her family relationships. Then she had to allow him to develop in her the attitudes that would lead to the eventual healing of her marriage.

Within a few months, Margaret's husband returned. Without the consistency of commitment, the magic of his moments of conquest faded and irritations led to a series of spats that dumped his whole affair. He returned to the creature comforts that he had spent half a lifetime building into a hearth and home.

There is a love unique to reconciliation that draws us deeper to the heart of God. Perhaps it is the tremor of self-doubt that builds our confidence only in his strength, and kneads us in the faith.

Margaret did not know how she would react to a second whack at the marriage bed.

"I put my trust in 1 Corinthians 7," she said. "Do not cheat each other of normal sexual intercourse, unless of course you both decide to abstain temporarily to make special opportunity for fasting and prayer. But afterwards you should resume relations as before, or you will expose yourselves to the obvious temptations of the devil" (Phillips translation).

Margaret abandoned her body to the ownership of her husband. Not only did she determine never again to deny him sexual intercourse, but she went a step further and initiated it frequently. It was a surprise to him. Her surprise was that she began to enjoy it.

"Three children into marriage," she said, "in the middle of the menopause, I learned how much fun sex can be when you actively go after it!"

"What about your husband's fidelity?" I asked. "He is an attractive man, in the swim of opportunity, aren't you concerned that he might have other affairs?"

"Yes," she frowned, "to be perfectly honest, I'm scared stiff. But I am learning to discipline my mind, rejecting what Paul calls vain imaginations. Instead of acting on my own fears and feelings, I have learned to set the priority of first acting on what I know and believe, through the scriptures, to be God's will for my marriage."

Margaret's husband is self-centered, body-proud, and goal-oriented. What he wants, he wants *now* and he works hard to get it. This means that sometimes she is pushed aside. He is not a Christian, which puts even more flexibility and spiritual focus on her.

She is learning how to love him differently. Her love has moved from *taker* to *giver*.

"I care for him and value his happiness to the point where, not just theoretically, but factually, through deliberate choice, it has become far more important to me than my own."

Her love is a growing, living, active, moving force.

What began in desperation is now building in confidence and mutual trust. Her marriage has moved up and out of *worse,* it is pushing through to *good,* and is getting *better* all the time.

The Spanish have a proverb, *"El prescuezo da vuelta a la cabeza":* "It is the neck that turns the head." In Margaret's case, she turned her husband's 180 degrees.

Love thrives on love. Love withers for want of love. Paul defines it with only active verbs. Love tolerates, is kind, is not jealous, nor self-centered. It is modest, good mannered, thinks the best, celebrates truth, believes, hopes, endures, never fails (1 Corinthians 13).

Love actively participates. It is sequential and progressive. It does not sit on its haunches and passively twiddle it's thumbs.

It has an environmental impact that can change any landscape.

On the occasion of his twentieth wedding anniversary, Jon Roe of the *Wichita Eagle & Beacon* wrote a tribute to his wife:

> Perfect marriages can't stand the strain of imperfect people. That's why you don't see any of them around for long. Had we sought the perfect marriage, we should have married people more fitting, and settled into one of those marriages that run on their own momentum.
>
> The "Let's Watch the Bulls Run at Pamploma" marriage in which the participants are constantly partying so they won't ever have to be alone together. Or the

"Old Dog Tray" marriage, in which each asks but one thing of the other—Don't ever surprise me.

But we fell into neither of those safe marriages, nor into the fatal "Push-Pull" type in which one partner grows while the other doesn't. Instead, we both had an awful lot of growing to do ... so much that we've been growing ever since, going through such changes that each of those 20 years has found us very different persons, and given us scores of opportunities to divorce. Luckily, each day of those 20 years, we've chosen each other all over again. That's 7,300 affirmative choices. Not a bad record.

But, had we started out perfect, we'd have had nothing to work on, nowhere to go and no one to be constantly fascinated by. You see, I may not know for certain just who you'll be from day to day ... but I know I'll be fascinated. Because I was lucky enough 20 years back to respond to some quality in you that I guessed would grow stronger over the years. Maybe that quality was simply your capacity for growth. Whatever it was, I've found that new person in my life each day at least as interesting, intriguing, charming and compelling as the one she replaces. I'm constantly fascinated."

Now that's *good,* that's the growing edge of *better,* that's moving up towards the very *best!*

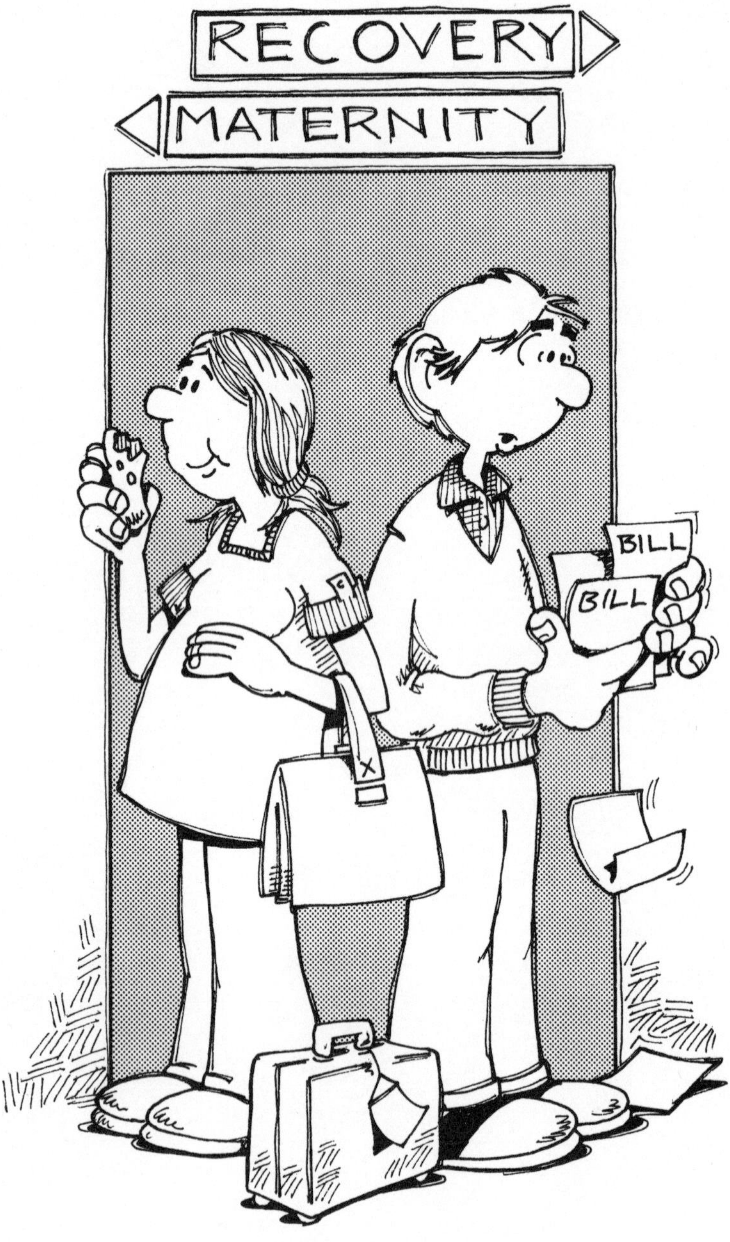
RECOVERY
MATERNITY
BILL
BILL

Motherhood, Apple Pie, & Other Irritations

Motherhood announces itself with a sinking feeling in the pit of the stomach and a craving for pickles. The craving for pickles eventually leaves, but the sinking feeling never quite goes away.

It is significant that our first biological response to being with child is the urge to throw up. It is also significant that shortly after delivery, some nine months later, the urge is to cry nonstop for several days, with the baby blues!

Obviously, our body knows something that we don't—namely, that on and off we will continue to have one or the other (or at times both) of these urges for much of our mothering lives.

This is confirmed all too soon as we pass through the terrible twos, the traumatic teens, and move along to the temperamental twenties ... sometimes known as the "you've come a long way baby" blues.

Fathers operate on a delayed reaction. They experience the urge to throw up the moment they change their first diaper, and the urge to cry nonstop when they get the obstetrician's bill, the pediatrician's bill, and the hospital bill. This gives many of them a disposition to name their baby "Bill" (or "Billie") with the same flourish of the pen that signs their checks. Little do they know that the orthodontist's bill and the college tuition bill are just around the corner, and that while one little hand is clutching their finger, the other little hand is reaching for their wallet.

The nesting instinct that woos us into the nursery pulls in tension against the stark terror of the responsibility to grow, mold, and finance another human being. We develop a worry-worry, stew-stew syndrome that comes from wondering whether we are doing all that we should as parents, and whether they are doing all that they should, or shouldn't (which is worse) as children.

The stress intensifies when we mirror our performance in Proverbs 22:6, "Train up a child in the way he should go and when he is old, he will not depart from it."

Although Solomon dug this thorn into our parental flesh, there is comfort in the fact that he does not say how old is "old."

Furthermore, as he was to find out with his son Rehoboam (who pranced through the pages of 1 Kings, and 2 Chronicles, with antics that made his name synonymous with folly, apostasy, and evil), training up a child in the way that he should go is easier said than done. And seeking divine intervention that he will not depart from it is what keeps parents on their knees and running to and from the confessional with furrows on their brows.

Solomon had seven hundred wives and three hundred concubines. This gives us the awesome statistic that, averaging one a night, it would have taken him nearly three years to make the rounds of all his women. In between, he managed to write three thousand proverbs and 1,005 songs. With proverbs outnumbering songs three to one, this goes to show he did not have quite as much to sing about as he did to warn and instruct about as a result of all his connubial bliss.

Missing the mark of much of his God-given spiritual wisdom, and having tragically departed from the training up of his own childhood, Solomon died at the relatively young biblical age of sixty-two, probably from sheer exhaustion and an overdose of ginseng.

There is no record of just how many children he had. Counting them, much less training them up, would have in itself been a laudable feat.

We do know that Rehoboam had twenty-eight sons and sixty daughters, and the scriptures tell us that he "dealt wisely with them," dispersing them throughout many countries. This seems practical and certainly far easier than keeping all eighty-eight of them at home and underfoot.

Coping with only two or three sons and daughters, there are many times when today's parents would like to deal wisely with their children by dispersing them throughout many countries . . . far away places, with strange-sounding names like Timbuktu and Lower Slobovia.

Instead of which they grit their teeth, pull out their Bibles, and memorize such verses as, "Spare the rod and spoil the child" (Proverbs 13:24), and, "This too shall pass" (Revelation 21:1).

The first test of training up a child comes on the toilet—the throne before which every mother kneels, cajoles, begs, whistles through her teeth, threatens, bribes, and wipes up.

Then, having spent two years of her baby's life in trying to get him to focus his attention on the performance of his private parts, she spends the next twenty-two years of his life trying to get him not to.

Unfortunately, one never knows in what likely or unlikely places training, or lack of it, may show up. When it does it inevitably reverts back to, "For goodness sake, didn't his *mother* teach him anything!"

This is one reason why so many mothers wear sunglasses and mumble a lot.

When our son was six years old we pushed him into the youth choir in the church. He wore a blue robe with a gold bow and stood in the front row. He had dark curly hair, large hazel eyes, and a toothless grin.

We called him "our pride and joy"—that is, until one memorable Sunday, during the singing of the second stanza of "All Things Bright and Beautiful." He developed an itch and decided to scratch. He scratched vigorously. The whole congregation averted their eyes and blushed, and the choir director turned pale.

Four hundred people buzzed the same thought, and it swarmed directly around my head: "Whose child is this?"

He was mine.

Suddenly, it did not seem to matter that he knew all ten of the commandments, or that he could recite John 3:16. Obviously, his training up had not included, "When you itch in public, don't scratch."

I have been wearing sunglasses and mumbling around the Sunday School ever since . . . so have his teachers.

As God's crisis intervention center, motherhood winces every time Dennis the Menace prays, "I got in a good fight with Tommy, Mr. Wilson chased me home again, and Margaret said she hates me. Thank you, Lord, for a perfect day!"

Teenage is a disease that only age will cure. From acne to algebra, it is the pit at the bottom of the rainbow, and the main cause of Excedrin headache numbers thirteen, fourteen, fifteen, and sixteen (years).

I was sitting in one of the off-studio waiting rooms discussing with the other members of the panel the various points each of us would make during an upcoming TV interview, when a young man walked in.

He was stunningly good looking, nicely dressed complete with the detail of every mother's fantasy— a shirt and tie. He was introduced to us as the teenage representative from one of the area high schools. His qualifications were a grade point average of 4.0, he was an Eagle Scout, and he had won several scholastic as well as Service Club awards. He was well-mannered and articulate.

He was the sort of son I had always imagined that *I* would have.

Instead, I had left mine that morning wearing a pair of his Dad's oversized trousers hitched up with suspenders, a white doctor's smock that he had picked up at a rummage sale, and with his naturally curly hair frizzed in an Afro to give him the Harpo Marx look.

It was "Spirit Day" at school and he was in top form. He would not talk, which could have been rather nice for a change, except that in reply to everything I said, he went "honk-honk" in my face with a large motor horn.

His room was clutter wall-to-wall and chances were that he had not quite finished his homework. That would mean yet another confrontation when his midterm grades came out. Expending only enough effort necessary to squeak him through the minimum required to stay on the football team, his major was pizza and girls, not necessarily in that order—a lot depended on the girl.

Had I taken him on the talk show that morning, he would have rolled his eyes and honk-honked his way through the interview. This would probably have won us a lot more points for our side than did our dialogue, and would have undoubtedly upped the ratings by at least 200 percent, but Little Lord Fauntleroy he was not!

The eleventh commandment is, "Thou shalt not covet thy neighbor's child."

As I mulled over the contrast between the desires of my mother's heart and the reality of the flesh of my flesh, I flipped through the pages of my Bible. Stuck opposite Proverbs 22 was a hand-drawn birthday card done when Ian was eight. It was a cartoon of Super-Mom, swinging from a trapeze—his scrawled greeting read, "MOM upside down is wow!"

Guilt misted my heart and I whispered, "Harpo Marx frizz, 2.0 grade point average, pizza and girls not withstanding . . . you're a little bit of all right, son!"

When it comes down to the nitty-gritty (and motherhood has more gritty in it than anything else, especially when she lives by the beach), MOM is the wow that melts the human heart.

Between the agony that is Howard Cosell and Monday Night Football is the ecstasy when the camera zooms in to a close up of a 250-pound tackle sipping Gatorade from a straw. He may belch and spit, and be the crunch of the defense, but when he looks into the TV lens, waves and says, "Hi Mom!" he is Little Boy Blue, and a time-out back to diaper pins, measles, detentions, and building the Alamo with toothpicks. Across the nation motherhood smiles, wipes a tear from her eyes, sits up a little straighter, and says, "Go for it, son!"

The fact of the matter is that the greatest national resource of a country is not the bullion in its banks, nor the trees in its forests, but the children in its homes.

Today's toddler wiping his nose on the living room drapes and sending his mother climbing the walls may be tomorrow's judge, pounding the gavel on the Supreme Court.

Whatever we may begin, or accomplish, our children will have the option to continue or destroy. The control of our political process, corporate power, education, church, and home, all pass into their hands. They will keep the peace or wage the war.

An investment in a child is an investment in tomorrow.

With human life as her product, and an estimated budget between $85,000 and $134,000 (from birth to age eighteen), motherhood comes into focus as an all-time high in professional calling.

Her options are many.

She may be part of the dwindling elite still able to stay within the confines of her traditional role, planting pansies and pushing the pram around suburbia. This gives her a full and flexible time span and is an ideal environment in which to grow and train up a child. Battling an inflation that makes the American dream of owning a home almost a two-income necessity, she may have to bite the economic bullet and tighten her family's belt, but this is a small trade-off against two little arms around her neck, hearing the first word, watching the first step, drying a tear-stained cheek, and building memories into every hour.

"After years in the work force I never thought I could endure just being at home with the baby," one mother told me, "but I love it! Who could guess that ten pink baby toes could be so alluring ... or nap time such a welcome relief! I don't want to miss a moment of these growing years and I'll sacrifice a lot rather than have to go back to work."

On the other hand, breaking the tie that has too long bound her to the kitchen sink, motherhood is emerging with a new image and proving that she can cope with the executive suite.

With a child on one hip and a career on the other, a generation of tiny tots are the new breed spoon-fed in the board rooms of major corporations or nursed in the family atmosphere of business facilities that have been specifically designed and staffed to accommodate the on-the-job-child. There is space for coffee break cuddles, nursing mothers, and lunchtime togetherness.

Her training him up may call for creative innovations that emphasize quality rather than quantity of time commitment, remote-control supervision, or manipulating her hours in the work force to coincide with his in school. But she is rising to the occasion and is effectively balancing her priorities.

Sometimes she has no choice, she has to—and with God's help, she can.

Kudos to fathers who respond positively to the custodial care of their children. One who was left with three ranging in age from twelve to three, said, "Problems? I prefer to think of them as the greatest opportunity of my life!" He rearranged his business hours, shuffled priorities, and did not merely cope— he enjoyed! So did his kids.

The *be*-attitudes of effective parenting are *be fair, be firm,* and *be fun.*

These are the guidelines used by Barbara Woodhouse, the international authority on the training of dogs. Not only will the dogs under her instruction go and fetch a stick or a ball, they will also *joyfully* go and fetch the choke collar with which she restrains and disciplines them.

If she can do it with Bowser, we can do it with Buster!

Be Fair

When my daughter was sixteen, after a family fracas, she stomped out of the room, tossed her head, and snapped, "The only reason I am still living at home is because of adolescence and poverty!"

I could not take credit for the adolescence, but thank heavens I had done something right in keeping her poor!

The golden rule around our house is, "He who has the gold makes the rule." Disbursing financial aid by way of weekly allowances, car keys, tanks full of gas, as well as the basic necessities of shelter, clothing, and food—our parental premise is, "As long as you are living under our roof and we are paying your bills, we will set the rules and you will need to keep them." Believing in the democratic process and fair play, we give our children the opportunity of sitting on the home-rule committee, and voting on final decisions. We keep the power of parental veto.

I grew up under the adage that children were to be seen and not heard, and I cannot remember the adults around me asking my opinion on anything apart from perhaps the color of a party dress. It was strictly, "Be quiet, sit down, and do as I say because

I say so with no questions asked." Or it was *the glare*—the evil eye that withered me on the spot!

I can still taste the bile of resentment and remember the tears of anger as I seethed, pounded my pillow at night and groaned, "It's not fair!"

As a result, I vowed that if ever I had children I would afford them the dignity of asking their opinion, and seriously considering their point of view in an open two-way communication.

One of the greatest gifts to a child is an ear, eager to listen. When stock broker E. F. Hutton speaks, the world may stop and listen, but when my kids speak, I stop and listen. Because I have very chatty kids, I have become a very good listener. I even listen when they don't know I'm listening . . . and that makes *them* seethe with anger, pound their pillows at night, and groan, "It's not fair!"

Conversely, when I talk I expect them to listen—not only with an eager ear, but with a focused eye. That way I can be sure that what I say is not going in one ear and out the other, but is taking at least a moment, however fleeting, to buzz around their heads.

Eye contact is one of the requirements in effective communication. Occasionally we stare each other down in silence, eyes blazing with anger, but . . . the first one who cracks up and smiles, wins!

For twelve years of their lives I was able to look down at them. Now in varying degrees, commensurate with their spurts of growth, they are able to look down at me—but whether it is up or down, even if we don't quite *see* eye to eye, at least we make the contact.

"Just because I say so" is not fair.

When a child is old enough to ask, he is old enough to know—on *any* subject. Perhaps not in full detail, but with sufficient explanation to make sense. If he does not get his answers from his parents, he will get them from someone else, and they may be the wrong answers.

My mothering services offer the short-form explanation, the come-and-sit-on-the-couch detailed explanation, or the deferred explanation ("We don't have time right now, but I will explain later.") Through the years I have become so expert in explanations that now in their behavior negotiations my children are apt to say, "Aw Mom, pleeze, I'm in a hurry—no explanations. Gimme a straight yes or no answer, or, 'just because you say so!'"

This is a foul aimed directly at my soap box.

When they are old enough to ask and they haven't, I do.

At sixteen my daughter started dating and I asked, "Have you set your sexual limits yet?"

"My what?" she squawked.

"How can you possibly go out," I said, "without knowing just what you will or will not let him do? He may touch you here, he may touch you there, he may try to touch you everywhere!"

She thought about it . . . for nearly two weeks. Then we talked about it for another two weeks, and on and off for another two years.

Considering her alternatives on her own, then talking them over in open (sometimes graphic) discussion, she eventually arrived at vital conclusions compatible with her Christian commitment. She now moves with confidence in the decisions that make her very much her own person, and not the pawn of her peers.

We tend to wear our children as badges of accomplishment—and that is not fair.

We glow at the thought of Stanford or Yale, and forget that Jesus went to Trade Tech—he was a carpenter.

We rate our children a spiritual ten if they stay in our faith, and marry in our faith, and twice times ten if they end up in the ministry or on the mission field. I spoke at a church once where, listed across the top of the Sunday bulletin, was the statement: "Pastor—every member of this church!" As ambassadors of Christ, every step that we take and every hand that we shake becomes our mission field.

If we are fundamental and our children turn ecumenical, or if we are ecumenical and they turn fundamental; or if they are charismatic, and we are not, and vice versa, we try to remember to say "Praise the Lord" in their church services, and hope they will remember not to say "Praise the Lord" in our church services, all of which is very hard on our spiritual arteries and keeps us balanced precariously on the edge of our Blessed Assurance.

If they smoke pot or "live in sin," their life scripts embarrass us; and if our church structure is built around 1 Timothy 3, we worry because we may get thrown off the board of deacons for not having our "children in subjection with all gravity." Obviously, Timothy forgot that Adam had Cain, David (who wrote the Psalms) had Absolom, and Jacob had ten raunchy sons who tried to kill their brother by throwing him down a well.

Far from doing everything right and living to regret it, the track record of many of the Patriarchs knocks them off their parental pedestal, and is a far cry from the admonition to be "sober, vigilant, the husband of one wife, and blameless."

Sorry Abraham, you flunked!

If, in spite of all our training up, our children end up marrying nonbelievers, we have a spiritual hot-flash and mutter things like "unequally yoked."

Some years ago, my life was touched during a lecture by Marianne Alireza, the first American woman to marry an Arabian prince and to be admitted to a harem.

She was not a Moslem and the Prince's family could have been devastated by the choice of their son to take an American bride—not of their race and not of their creed. As Marianne arrived at her new home and stepped out of the limousine in front of the palace, instead of being cold and haughty, her mother-in-law came flying down the steps, flung her arms around her, and said, "*Because my son loves you, I will love you too!*"

That is what God the Father says to me.

That is what I pray I will be able to say to whoever my children chose to marry, and I intend to mean it and live it with all my heart.

We love, but on whose terms?

We hope it will be with the unconditional love that wrote in the sand, "Let he that is without sin among you cast the first stone."

Be Firm

Maureen was fifteen. She was what my husband called a "spirited child." That was a nice way of saying she was stubborn, self-willed and a holy terror who wreaked havoc in her family circle. She was very pretty and had a charming coyness when she chose, which I suspect is why my husband was so kindly disposed towards her. Had she been ugly, he probably would have called her a spoiled brat.

Having been something of a spoiled brat myself, I liked Maureen. She had taught my daughter how to "sex" a guinea pig (tell the difference between male and female—no easy task!), and she had given us her three hens, Tasha, Rhoda, and Hilda, when her interest advanced from collecting eggs as a daily hobby to collecting boys as a weekly hobby. Whether she could distinguish the good eggs from the rotten eggs in the boys as easily as she could in the hens remained to be seen. Reports had it that she couldn't, and that was what was making her family very queasy.

After years of loneliness, her mother was getting married again. We were thrilled. But who would keep Maureen during the honeymoon? She had a reputation of climbing out of her bedroom window in order to keep a forbidden nocturnal rendezvous—she certainly could not be trusted to stay by herself. Her aunts and uncles were all somewhat intimidated by her, and were very nervously disposed towards her.

We volunteered, and invited her to move in with us for the ten-day period.

"Give us her schedule and a list of her dos and don'ts." we asked. "Set the ground rules with her, and let *her* set the penalty for breaking them ... then have her sign the list!"

Maureen arrived like a lamb and we expected that within twenty-four hours she would be a roaring lion.

We posted her list on the refrigerator door, and the children, several years younger than she was, had eyes as round as saucers as they helped drag in her stereo and speakers. She won them over immediately by letting them take turns in listening through the earphones. When I asked for a turn, she took great delight at my grimace and scream of pain as I felt my brains being blasted out of the top of my head. Without the earphones, we could not have made it through the week; with earphones, I felt we had a chance.

Monday, Wednesday, Friday, and Saturday nights were her nights out—she had a curfew of midnight. Monday night we watched her primp and blow-dry her hair, then shook the hand of the gawky boy who came to pick her up.

"I'm going to sleep," I told her, "but I will set the alarm to wake me at 11:45 just so I can be sure you're home on time."

"You don't have to do that," she said sweetly.

"Oh yes I do," I said sweetly.

"What do you care?" she challenged.

"I do care," I said. "Enough to check that you made it home safely and on time. Besides, maybe we can even have a late-night cup of tea together!"

Both Monday and Wednesday she was home in good time. Friday night the alarm went off at 11:45—I put the kettle on and waited. At 11:55, still no Maureen. I peered through the drapes, clock in hand, and prayed with every ticking second, "Hurry her home, Lord." More than anything, I didn't want to have to punish her. Grounding her would probably set her off in such bad temper that it would be harder on me than on her!

At 11:59, Maureen's clock started to bong a countdown in the last minute to midnight. I was pacing the floor—suddenly, headlights screeched into the driveway, a slight girl with her long hair flying like a thoroughbred straining to the finish line dashed up the front steps, turned the key in the lock and fell into my waiting arms. We hugged and I giggled, "Where is your glass slipper, Cinderella?"

I told her how tempted I was to turn back the clock to get her off the hook.

The tears came into her eyes. "Would you do that just for me?" she asked.

"Yes," I said, "I would do practically anything just not to have to punish you. I'm for you, not against you, but we must keep the rules."

We talked a lot that week. I learned about the rotten egg boys and the good egg boys. We had pizza for breakfast, or leftover curry stuffed into pita bread pockets. Every morning she would rush in and say, "What's for breakfast today?"

We out-outraged each other, and tried to out-love each other.

We broke a few traditional molds and ran our imaginations along the hours of that week to burst joy into every bright new day.

John was right, she was a "spirited child," bored with the commonplace, fired by the adventure of the new.

Some rules are fixed, immovable, where parents stand back-to-back so that the child cannot squeeze in between them like the stuffing in a sandwich, and use one as lever against the other. These rules are kept and the penalty firmly exercised, come hell or high water, despite howls and yowls, or slamming doors, or biting words.

Some rules are made for stretching.

We have programmed into our family disciplines a "way of escape."

Paul tells us, "There hath no temptation taken you but such as is common to man; but God is faithful, who will not suffer you to be tempted above that ye are able; but will with the temptation also make a way to escape, that ye may be able to bear it" (1 Corinthians 10:13).

Reacting rather than responding, may God forgive me for the many times I have punished my children as a result of my own short temper and frustration, rather than in proportion to their transgression.

The cardinal sin of parenting is expecting our children to be adults. Some penalties, seemingly simple, are just too much for them to bear.

John and I decided that when our children needed a firm discipline, we would offer them a choice of alternatives, or an opportunity to "earn" their way out, as a way of escape.

We have a "redemption" bottle with chores written on slips of paper folded up inside—these may be pulled and done to modify a punishment.

When the children were little, so were the chores—as they grew, so did the tasks. Sometimes I would drop in an assignment such as, "Write an essay on why obscenity is socially unacceptable," or "Table manners are necessary—agree, or disagree?" Got them thinking! My son would generally stick with the punishment after pulling one of those, but my daughter would usually opt for the essay. Once she wrote a marvelous piece on "The Value of Housework, as it relates to God's order in the universe." Made even me want to pick up the broom and get busy!

Occasionally I would put in a slip that read, "Surprise! You're off the hook for free. One kiss will clear the slate—and see that it doesn't happen again." Like the dad who made a way of escape by rolling up his newspaper, taking junior to his room, then whispering, "Now you yell, while I wallop the chair."

All too often *firm* becomes *harsh*—that bitter root with its bitter fruit.

We push away in anger instead of pull towards in love.

Betsy was on heroin. She was prostituting herself in order to get the money for her fix, and she was caught in the worst of all possible worlds.

"If only I could go home," she wept.

She could not. Her family had thrown her out and slammed the door shut.

"Oh God," I prayed, "no matter what they do, please help me to always keep an open heart and an open home to our kids." The alternative is pushing them in to the street.

As the young prostitutes, some of them just eleven or twelve years old, go through Covenant House in the middle of New York City, Father Bruce Ritter calls their parents.

He twists up in grief as, all too frequently, he hears, "We don't want her home—you can keep her there!" He tries to modify the hurt as he translates, "Your parents say it's OK for you to stay here with me for a while." The child knows . . . she is not fooled.

My heart broke as I watched a TV special that showed a young man phoning home from the streets of Hollywood.

"Mom, I want to come home," he said.

"No," she said stoically, "you can't."

"Lady," I screamed at the television, "don't send

him back on the street! Do you know what it is like for a boy to turn ten tricks a night?" I wanted to shout, "Come here, son!"

Father Ritter says that for the kids on the street, the saddest day in the year is not Christmas, Thanksgiving, or Easter . . . it is Mother's Day.

Be Fun

Each New Year the members of our immediate family exchange resolutions—that means I give three and I get three. Correction, I only get two. . . . My husband usually kisses me and says, "I wouldn't dare improve on perfection!" And that makes me tear up the one I had prepared for him, which is very aggravating, as I have usually spent the entire year plotting just what I would give him.

My son is liable to get, "Improve your grades this year without being nagged." And he is liable to give, "Don't nag me to improve my grades this year."

My daughter gives hers out in a sealed envelope with little green unicorns stamped all over it. Mine generally reads, "Dear Mom, I love you, but . . ." there follows not one, but some fifteen possible resolutions that are her way of saying, "These are the things you do that bug me half to death."

Imagine my delight the year her note read:

Dear Mother:

In the past I have been frustrated with you. Now I want to commend you.

You have been much more comfortable when I practice my driving, and I have noticed that. You are not critical and are very accepting of my friends. You have been kind to them, and I am beginning to believe those nice things they say about you behind your back.

I realize that mothering is very difficult, and I just want to commend you on the excellent progress you have made during this past year.

I love you very much.

Anne

And that made me tear up the one I had for her!

Humor is the tilt of the soul that keeps us looking up even though we may be feeling down.

Using family fun as a safety valve through which to blow off steam, we work out the kinks that tend to stiffen up the joints linking us together. We have learned to laugh at ourselves and with each other, and to develop family jokes and traditions that will probably carry on through many generations.

We went through a siege of chicken pox with two balls of green yarn. I suggested to the children that they web their rooms and when they were through, they could entice me in, like the spider to the fly, and see whether I could meander through the maze. From the bedpost, through the loops in the wagon-wheel lamp, on to the latch on the window, back to the doorknob ... I do not think there was a drawer or cupboard pull that escaped their innovative spin. We climbed our way in and out for days and ended up shooting paper airplanes into the webbing. Chicken pox was fun!

Summertime is for eating strawberries dripping with cream, and wind-whipped walks along the shore.

I slam my typewriter shut, put my brain on hold, and tie on an apron. I become Little Red Hen, packing picnic baskets and washing thousands of towels.

"Who will dust the living room?" I ask.

"Not I," says the son, "I have a part-time job."

"Not I," says the daughter, "I have a date."

"I will, I will," says the Little Red Hen, and she does.

"Who will fold the laundry?" asks the Little Red Hen.

"Not I," says the son, "I am completely bushed."

"Not I," says the daughter, "my nails are still wet."

"I will, I will," says the Little Red Hen, and she does.

When Little Red Hen gets to the Pearly Gates, Saint Peter will take her by her worn-out feathery wing and say, "Well done, my good and faithful Little Red Momma Hen, come and sit in the eternally clean room I have prepared for you where there is no more dusting, or folding, and you may eat strawberries and cream for the next two thousand years!"

"Nonsense!" says a friend of mine. "Saint Peter will take you by the wing and say, 'Stupid Little Red Momma Hen, you did not train up your children in the way that they should go, to help you with the chores. Go and dust the halos and fold the angel wings for the next two thousand years!'"

Traditions are the pearls that space the beads of memory and ornament our lives.

Not having much luck with apple pie (apples irritatingly undercooked, piecrust irritatingly overcooked!) the sweet-smelling savor that comes out of our kitchen is Christmas cake.

As legend has it, it all began in the little town of Tisdale, Saskatchewan, when great-grandfather Angus came over from Scotland and great-grandmother Collins came over from Ireland. They met and they married and they began to propagate the earth, as many of their kith and kin across the Canadian prairies will testify. But whether it was because of his Scottish thrift and they did not go out and spend much, or because of her Irish temper and they did not sit down and talk much, or whether it was just because it was forty degrees below zero in Tisdale, Saskatchewan and there was not much else to do but shiver, they decided to bake a Christmas cake.

Some 3,640 walnuts, 10,112 raisins, and several other thousands of ingredients of fruit and nuts later, to say nothing of the spices and cups of brandy (both in the cake and in great-grandfather, which is probably why he suggested it in the first place) later, the famous Angus fruitcake recipe was perfected.

It became part of the tradition of their clan to pass along the recipe for the cake to every new bride, together with one for haggis, cock-a-leekie, and Irish soda bread. I received mine, neatly packaged in a tartan recipe box, with the motto, "What food these morsels be!"

In the first year of our marriage, the genes from his great-grandfather started jumping in my husband, and with one eye on the brandy bottle and the other on the recipe box, he decided that we should establish our own tradition by making the famous cake. Had he chosen the haggis (cooked in a sheep's paunch), he would not have enjoyed a second year of marriage.

Not having a bowl big enough in which to mix the fifteen pounds of assorted fruit and nuts, we decided to mix it in the kitchen sink. Unfortunately, the sink was not stopped up well enough and most of the brandy was lost down the drain, which made ours the driest fruitcake this side of Carrie Nation—a terrible hardship on any Scot, but obviously the nemesis of God.

After our babies were born we immediately decided to include them in our Christmas cake tradition by mixing it in their plastic bath tub. This worked wonders for retaining all the moisture, but lent a distinct flavor of Johnson's baby soap to the cake. It also lent a distinct aroma of brandy to the babies' bathwater, which is probably one of the reasons they smiled so much during early infancy.

As the children grew, it was their part of the continuing tradition to collect all ten eggs needed for the cake from Tasha, Rhoda, and Hilda, so that we could say that they were fresh-laid from Angus hens.

We said "fresh" based, of course, on the day that they were found, not necessarily on the day that they were laid. As the hens changed their nest from day to day, it sometimes took the children several weeks to find the fresh-laid eggs—and by that time they were piled so high it was impossible to miss them.

Running free and nourished with the best slugs, snails, worms, earwigs, and sow bugs that our garden could produce, our hens lay organic eggs, which we then process into our organic cake. However, we would prefer the organisms found in the cake not be examined under a microscope as the Department of Health might abort our family Christmas tradition.

Sometimes we encourage the children to put lucky dimes into the cake. This means you are especially lucky if they don't crack a bicuspid crown, or gum up the works in the garbage disposal. As it is part of the tradition to make a wish with the first bite of cake every Christmas, we ask our guests to make the wish before they bite, as after they bite they may wish they had never bitten, thus wasting a perfectly good wish.

When we raise our children on a lap full of laughter, we program into them the merry heart that Solomon says is a "continual feast" (Proverbs 15:15).

It will nourish them all their lives.

How to Get Up on Your Down Days

I have enough trouble trying to get up on my *up* days, much less on my *down* days! Most days I'd rather not get up at all. As the first glimmer of light breaks through the fuzz of morning, I search frantically for my pulse, just to be sure I'm still alive. I roll out of bed, stagger to the bathroom mirror, take one look at the puffy eyes, tousled hair, bleak pallor of my natural self, and gasp, "Good grief, do I have to depend on *you* to get me through another day?"

The fact of the matter is, yes I do, and the motivational question is *how*?

Hubert Humphrey knew how.

His father taught him step one of affirmative action: *get up!* "Stay out of bed as long as you can. Most people die there. You are only alive when you are awake."

Humphrey went on to develop a zest for life that never left him. It won him the reputation of being an evangelist of benevolence, and a chronic enthusiast. When he died, his colleagues eulogized: "He taught us how to win, how to lose, how to live, and now he has taught us how to die."

Humphrey won, lost, lived, and died enthusiastically! It was not only chronic, it was contagious—it reached out to infect those with whom he came in contact.

Enthusiasm was the buoyancy that tossed him up and floated him over the storms in his life. It was the glue that held together the shattered pieces of his varied experiences, and enabled him to carry on with fortitude and vigor.

Now the tah-rah-rah-boom-dee-ay of "everything's going my way," is an anthem easy to toot. It is the win syndrome of successful living. But when the chips are down, in this case even to the point of death itself, the ability to maintain an unmitigated enthusiasm reflects an essence of being that stretches far beyond the norm of human capacity.

"I have done my best. I have lost. Mr. Nixon has won. The democratic process has worked its will, so now let's get on with the urgent task of uniting our country."

Humphrey wrote that, "In a lifetime of thousands of speeches and millions of words, those were the hardest ones I have ever had to speak."

Yet his sense of national priority lifted him *up* and over the disappointment of personal defeat. His "let's get on with it ..." stirred a motivational enthusiasm that fired him up for what he called the "art of the possible."

Poignantly, on the final Christmas day that tolled his coming death, his thoughts went to the man who beat him out of the White House.

Nixon sat exiled in the post-Watergate loneliness

of San Clemente. Cognizant of his own rundown on the clock, Humphrey phoned, and dipping into the reservoirs of his magnanimous heart he extended, with compassionate memory, his warm seasonal greetings. Although bitter antagonists on the political platform, he broke through the veneer of Nixon's cold personality to clasp him in the grip of the most equalizing of human need—mutual suffering.

This parting tribute embodied his philosophy that, "no matter how high a man may rise in this democracy, he functions with the human emotions and limitations that we all share."

In his final days, those limitations wracked Humphrey's body and pinioned him as a monument to his own articulate truth.

During one particularly difficult bout with chemotherapy, his liver was injected, directly.

"I just wanted it all to end .... The pain was just too much to bear. I couldn't catch my breath. Every bone in my body ached," he confided to his doctor, Edgar Berman, "but ... a man just has to count his blessings!"

At the tag end of his battle with cancer, those blessings had dwindled down to gratitude for the ability to digest one spoonful of cereal—a taste of Special K.

"But ..." Humphrey said cheerfully, "a week ago I couldn't even face a cracker."

The word enthusiasm has as its root the Greek *en theos*, meaning "in God." Humphrey's enthusiasm was rooted in his faith in God, in America, and the political process, and in the intense commitment of his life. A gut-level confidence that enabled him to be "an optimist—without apology!"

His directionals revolved around a simple slogan: "Life is to be enjoyed, not merely endured."

Jesus Christ said the same thing. He told us that he came that we might have life, and that we might have it "more abundantly" (John 10:10).

If our life is a dull shade of tattle-tale grey, Jesus came to brighten it up. If our life is shattered, he came to put it back together again. If our life is empty, he came to fill it. And if our life is bountiful, he came to bring it even more abundance.

He points us to the crux: "These things have I told you, so that *my joy* might remain in you, and that *your joy* might be full" (John 15:11).

How full is our joy?

In making the clear differential between his joy and ours, Jesus zeros in on the essential priority— first his, before ours can ever be full.

Our joy, which has its frustrating dependence on all that we are, on the interaction of our relationships with those around us, and on the circumstances of our environment, weighed in counterpoint perspective against God's joy, dependent on all that Jesus is. This is the differential that transcends the limitations of our finite capacity with the infinite resource of the Godhead to translate and empower our lives.

In the back of my Bible, I have written these words:

If I look at myself I am depressed.

If I look at those around me I am often disappointed.

If I look at my circumstances I am discouraged.

If I look at Jesus Christ, I am constantly, consistently, and eternally fulfilled.

Years ago, a friend used that little verse to develop in me a tunnel-vision to Jesus Christ.

If We Look at Ourselves . . .

Our bookshelves are lined with all that we are, all that we aren't, and all that somebody else thinks we should be. *How to Be Your Own Best Friend, I'm OK—You're OK,* or *I'm OK—You're Not So Hot!*

With psychologists pumping self-images into us, with theologians translating concepts at us, with all the information we have at our fingertips, somehow we still do not seem to be able to live up to our own, much less anyone else's, expectations. We are part of the "I blew it again" consequence of finite performance.

When Ian was seven years old, I came into the house one day and found him reading a magazine he had no business looking at nor bringing into our home.

He was born one hot August night under the smoggy light of the full California moon. This gave him a predisposition to yowl long and hard until he was blue in the face, or until he got his own way, whichever came first (usually blue in the face).

He greeted the world "butts-up" in a breech delivery, and one look at his mass of dark hair creeping half way down his neck told me that his hormones would be jumping long before puberty.

We thought about calling him Esau (the hairy one), but were afraid it might predict the selling of his birthright for a bowl of porridge; a natural temptation, porridge being the birthright and yen of any good Scot by the name of Angus.

Instead, we called him Ian—the classic, Gaelic form of John, "the beloved."

He was a winsome lad, with a merry heart and a twinkle in his eye. He had a smile that could sell snow to the Eskimos, and a wanderlust that took him on escapades around the neighborhood—enough to put patience and long-suffering into any mother's life. Whether there was too much lust to his wander, or too much wander to his lust, we have yet to find out; but at age three, after spending the afternoon with one of his playmates, I got a call from her mother.

"My daughter is in the bathtub, and I want you to know that your son has drawn a happy face on her bare bottom!"

"Hold on a jiff," I squeaked in panic, as I rushed to take a look at Ian, splashing around in our tub. "Sure 'nuff," I breathed in hilarious relief, "your daughter has drawn a happy face on my son's bare bottom."

The grin-and-share-it of a camaraderie sealed with the mark of childhood innocence.

Fortunately, the happy faces were both smiling. Unfortunately, they were drawn in indelible ink.

Now, four years later, I was not smiling as I confronted him, caught with the graphic evidence of a *Playboy* centerfold.

He put his hands over his ears and said, "Hear no evil . . ." his hands over his mouth and said, "Speak no evil . . ." then he grinned sheepishly, shrugged his shoulders and said, "Two out of three ain't bad!"

He hit the mark to pinpoint where most of us are. It is not that we go about serializing sin through our lives (although some of us do!). It is just our simple failure to measure up to all that we know we should be. For the most part, we are a "two out of three ain't bad" people.

We get depressed.

The fact of the matter is that life is only as good as our disposition—that is what sold Carter's Little Liver Pills in the forties, and that is what has our national statistic at 3.2 *billion* valium tablets consumed annually.

We are a hurting people.

What generally hurts us are other people.

Lack of other people sometimes hurts us more. It is called the stark terror of loneliness. Lonely is one of the few words in our language that does not have a word to express its opposite. We are either lonely, or we are not.

An experience that intersected the complacency of my status quo and enlarged the peripheral vision of my heart was the day I held in my arms the sobbed-out anguish of a woman devastated by loneliness.

She was parched for affection and the simple milk

of human kindness. She had reached a breaking point.

"Sometimes I go into my hall closet," she cried in desperation, "and I tug on the coats and jackets hanging there—'Talk to me,' I beg them, 'please, talk to me!'"

"Oh God," I prayed, "put our arms into those empty sleeves and teach us how to wrap them around each other!"

I have always felt a strange affinity for those who move on the fringes of our culture. Drifting in and out of our lives are "angels of opportunity."

Sophie walked around the town in white ankle socks, sandals and a short knitted cape that turned whatever dress she may choose to wear into a uniform. She dyed her hair, but not often enough, so that dark roots streaked through garish red. She lived alone, with no one to talk to, and no one to care. She was arrogantly loquacious, which gave one the tendency to cross the street rather than become entrapped in one of her long conversations. She sniffed a lot.

When she started coming to church I sought her out, and sat next to her, delighted with the opportunity to let the outrage of her style rub me with a new dimension.

When she sniffed and people looked back, I handed her a kleenex. "Thanks," she'd say, and blow her nose. One day I didn't have a kleenex, so I just started sniffing with her. If people were going to scowl and stare, they could—at both of us!

After the service, she generally walked to the local market, bought a sandwich from the deli, and sat on the bench outside, watching cars full of family and friends drive home. I had the odd feeling that she was an observer from some strange galaxy, sent to analyze our hearts.

As we drove past, Sunday after Sunday, on our way home to a dinner, ample to share, I wanted to invite her to come ... but I never did, and I wish I had. She's gone now. God alone knows where. She left my horizon, and I feel the pain of an empty sleeve into which I never put my arm.

Depression is not to be taken lightly. Frequently, it is the symptom of what might be a severe illness, and needs clinical diagnosis and treatment.

But sometimes all it calls for is a good shot of estrogen, or a run around the block, or several slams on the tennis court to work out a stress. For the most part, our depression stems from a bad case of the blahs. The saggy, baggy, down-in-the-mouth feeling that has us dive under the bedclothes, pull the covers up over our heads, and whine, "Pass me by, world, I don't want to get on!"

One emotionally drenched day, when I was caught in the ebb tide of my own frustrations, I sat wrapped in the colorful squares of an heirloom afghan, watching an interview with Golda Meir over Public Broadcasting.

"Do you ever feel depressed about the State of Israel?" she was asked, "Do you get pessimistic?"

She had seen six million Jews march to Hitler's

crematoriums, many chanting the anthem of their faith, *Ani ma'amin be'emuna shlema beviat ha-Mashiah* ("I believe with perfect faith in the coming of the Messiah"). She had groaned in agony at reports of the atrocities. She had wrestled for a lifetime with the right of her nation to exist.

Yet in retrospect, she noted, "Emotional stamina is mostly a matter of habit, and whatever else we lacked, we did not lack opportunities for testing ourselves in times of crisis. . . . One can always push oneself a little bit beyond what only yesterday was thought to be the absolute limit of one's endurance."

Now her dark eyes were flashing at mine through the television camera. Her answer whipped my spirit.

"The State of Israel, the Israeli people," she said, "cannot afford to take the time to feel pessimistic or depressed about anything, because the Israeli people have too much to do!"

So do we.

Each of us has been curiously and carefully made (some more curiously than others!). We have been individually programmed and finely tuned for the specific opportunity of God working in and through our lives. We are his instruments of purpose.

Stradivari made instruments—among the finest in the world. George Eliot wrote:

> When any master holds
> 'Twixt chin and hand a violin of mine,
> He will be glad that Stradivari lived,
> Made violins and made them of the best.

For while God gives them skill
I give them instruments to play upon,
God choosing me to help Him . . .
If my hand slacked
I should rob God—since He is fullest good—
Leaving a blank instead of violins.
He could not make Antonio Stradivari's violins
Without Antonio!

If our hands slack, they should rob God. He puts purpose into our lives when our lives are committed to his purpose.

A young son was asked to give the blessing at the dinner table one night. He thanked God for the food, then paused, and added, "And thank you, God, for the neat little brother you gave this family."

"Neat little brother?" his father asked, "Where?"

"Right here," said the son, pointing to himself, "I mean me!"

He was on target—we need to thank God for ourselves. Not for the flubs that we make, nor for the flabs that we might be becoming, but for all the possibilities he has in working through our lives. We all come tagged: "With the compliments of your Creator!"

If I Look at Those Around Me . . .

Been disappointed lately? By a spouse? A child? Children, plural? Or perhaps a close friend unintentially breaking a confidence? A mother-in-law?

Or maybe you and I, as that close friend or mother-in-law, have disappointed someone else. What is worse than someone disappointing us is the awful, anguished realization that we have been the source of someone else's disappointment.

After speaking at a retreat in California, a beautiful white-haired lady came to the foot of the podium. There were tears in her eyes and on her face was a twisted expression of grief.

"I am the pastor's mother-in-law," she said. "And I have been such a terrible disappointment to him and to my family. I have been a complainer, a meddler, and a trouble-maker. I have been disruptive. I have made his ministry difficult, and . . . oh, I am so sorry!"

As she broke down and sobbed, her daughter, the pastor's wife, stepped down from the platform where she had been standing beside me. She reached out, and with the tears welling up in her own eyes, she hugged her mother and cried, "Oh Momma, I forgive you!"

The magic words—two of the most healing words in our vocabulary, "I'm *sorry*," and "I *forgive* you."

A few years ago, this saying made the rounds; "Love is never having to say you're sorry."

Baloney.

Love is saying you're sorry—love is saying you're sorry over and over again, and then one more time, just to make sure. Love is saying you're sorry even when it is not your fault.

That is what Jesus did. He hung there on the cross . . . "I'm sorry, my Father. I'm sorry for the sins of the world. I'm sorry for all those things that Fay does that she shouldn't do. For all those things that she thinks that she shouldn't think. For all those things that she says that she shouldn't say. I'm sorry!"

He was sorry unto death.

Some of the most tension-filled times in our family occur during the dinner hour. What I call the "jowl and scowl" time. These lead to knots in our tummies and massive cases of indigestion. They frequently occur because no one is willing to say "I'm sorry." No one is willing to take the blame.

"I'm not going to say 'I'm sorry,'" snorts my son; "it's all her fault, she started it!"

"Huh—listen to Mr. Big over there," snarls my daughter, "why should I say I'm sorry for something I didn't do!"

I see the muscles in my husband's face twitching, and his jaws moving faster and faster as he bolts down his food. I think, "Good grief, he's changing from Winnie-the-Pooh into Hitler, and we're going to have an explosion!"

"Now listen here," I say, "I don't care whose fault it is. *I* will take the blame, *I* will say 'I'm sorry' for both of you. Just see to it that you've learned a lesson and that it doesn't happen again."

Oh the bumbles of our bitter pride that snuffs out the joy in each other when all the while our hearts are lonely to be loved.

The second most healing word in our vocabulary is, "I *forgive* you."

"Father, forgive them . . ." Jesus prayed.

Billy Graham once said that he believed in patting a kid on the back if the pat was low enough and hard enough to do some good.

When my daughter was eight I had a rare occasion to pat her on the back, good and low and hard!

She developed the art of plea bargaining at an early age, and became adroit at negotiating her options. If threatened with a punishment, she would want to know exactly what kind, for how long, and if she had the choice of substitute timing, or redemption.

If I caught her doing something she shouldn't, I'd say, "Stop it, or I'll swat you!"

"Where?" she would ask, and "how hard?" to weigh, not whether the punishment fit the crime, but rather whether the crime was worth the punishment. By the time she got through a manipulative dialogue, chances were I'd lost track of what it was all about. A strategy that should qualify her for a career in politics, or as an investigator for the IRS.

On this occasion, I bent her over my knee. With every whack she yelled, "I forgive you! I forgive you! I forgive you!" (The things they teach those kids in Sunday school.)

Now one doesn't paddle hard nor long when a child is yelling, "I forgive you!" with every whack. I don't remember her transgression, but maybe I did need her forgiveness, and she gave it immediately, without even waiting for me to say, "I'm sorry!"

I have a friend who wrestled with a very severe option of forgiveness when her beautiful daughter was brutally murdered.

The young husband returned home from work at

about four in the afternoon and found the body of his wife lying in a pool of blood at the foot of their baby's cot. Her last moments in life were the desperate effort of trying to reach her baby.

The authorities estimated that she died at about ten in the morning, which meant that the little child lay unattended in his crib for some six hours—surrounded, I'm sure, by the angels of mercy.

The funeral of that young girl was an inspiring celebration of placing her eternal life in the arms of Jesus.

Some weeks later, her mother and I were at a Bible study together, talking about forgiveness.

"I can accept the fact that my daughter is dead, and is with the Lord," she said, "but I cannot accept the way in which she died. I wake up sobbing, with nightmares—graphic dreams of brutality. Don't ask me to forgive her murderer."

"No," I replied. "I don't have the right to ask you to forgive anybody. All I can do is show you the alternatives of nonforgiveness—the development of a root of bitterness springing up in your life; resentment, depression, anger, perhaps even revenge. These will hurt you and could grow in intensity to eat their way through your disposition."

She chose to forgive the murderer, and she prayed for him. It is not very difficult to forgive people when you are praying for them. The healing of her memories began, and her nightmares stopped.

More difficult than forgiving others is the ability to forgive ourselves. But if Jesus forgives us, the least we can do is forgive ourselves.

After I spoke at a conference on this message, a pretty young woman sought me out. Tearfully, she told the story of her young husband's tragic illness and death.

"A year ago, I was attending a retreat at this very same spot. My husband phoned to tell me that he wasn't feeling well and pleaded with me to come home."

She took a deep breath, "I needed to get away so badly. It seemed that I was the one being buried, day after day, coping with the physical and emotional drain of his illness—it was wearing me out. When he called, I exploded with resentment and pent-up anger, to think that he couldn't even spare me one weekend in which to restore my spirit and strengthen my soul."

"I'm not going to tell you the mean things I said to him," she sobbed, "but I didn't drop everything and run home. I even hung up on him. A few weeks later, he died. I have never been able to forgive myself."

She took forgiveness, and as we prayed together she entered into the blessed peace and joy of casting off a burden she had no need to carry.

If I Look at My Circumstances . . .

Shortly after my first book was published, I had a letter from a girl in Arizona. She had come to the end of her rope—she was at a point of despair and discouragement where she felt it would be a lot easier to die rather than to live.

She had been through a traumatic divorce and had three small children. She was a born-again Christian, and attended an evangelical church.

She met a charming man at Sunday school, who professed to be a Christian. She felt that he was an answer to her loneliness and to her prayers. They were married.

Within one year, he had taken her financially for all that she had, and had left. She came down with a debilitating illness and was flat on her back for months, struggling to keep her small family going. She was so down, she could not even look up, much less get up!

Together, we went to the twenty-third Psalm.

"Yea, though I go through the valley of the shadow of death . . ."

Sometimes the valley of the shadow of life is more difficult than the valley of the shadow of death.

The key word in that psalm is "through." David did not say, Yea, though I *live* in the valley of the shadow. . . ." The going *through* is a moving, walking experience.

That girl had been ambushed in a valley; she pitched her tent there and stayed—trapped by the steep slopes of her own discouragement.

Slowly, with the help of the people from her church, she started moving. She would take two steps forward, and slip one step backward. She crept and crawled her way *through* the devastating circumstances of her life. Her brethren in Christ roped themselves together, like mountain climbers, to pull and tug her up and out. The cords binding them were not only prayer, but the practical gift of help.

It is a gift that we do not hear talked about much,

yet it is a gift that none of us can do without. A cup of cold water, a warm dinner, a $5 bill tucked into a cheery note, a drive to the doctor's office, children kept for a few hours. Lights shining through the end of a tunnel when everything within it is dark and gloomy.

That girl not only got up when she was flat down, but the last I heard from her she was working in a special facility, using her experience to help disturbed young women "make it *through*."

How I thank God that there is not a bleak experience in our lives that he cannot use for his purposes and glory!

An executive from World Vision taught me a marvelous definition of the word "experience."

A young man who was impressed with the efficiency of that outstanding organization, and the way the executive handled an international staff whose purpose was to ease the suffering of hurting people around the world, asked, "How did you manage to pull all this together and get it running smoothly?"

"Two words," said the executive. "Right decisions."

"Ah," said the young man, "but how did you come to make the right decisions?"

"One word," thundered the executive, "EXPERIENCE."

"How did you get the experience?"

"Two words," said the executive, "Wrong decisions!"

The wrong decisions that clobber us *down*, processed through our experience and the commitment of our faith, can be the turning points that pull us *up* and over the humps in our lives.

When I Look to Jesus Christ . . .

. . . I am constantly, consistently, and eternally fulfilled.

We have the promise of *his presence* that will never leave us, nor forsake us, but will be with us, always.

We have the promise of *his love,* that no power, terrestrial, nor extraterrestrial; no event in the past nor yet to come; life, nor even death itself, will ever be able to separate us from.

We have the promise of *his joy*—that spiritual condition that may not change the circumstances, but changes us, and fills us with a calm beyond our understanding. A peace that puts its confidence in the sovereignty of God to superintend our lives, and work "all things" together for our good, so that though the tears may be streaming down our faces and our hearts may be shattering into a thousand pieces, we are still able to look *up* and sing, "Great is Thy Faithfulness, O God, My Father!"

We enter into that supernatural joy by abiding in Christ. Jesus set the priority, "Abide in me"—first— then, "I in you" (John 15:4).

When we abide in someone, we live within their environment. We move into their home, so to speak. One of the first things we do when we live with someone is communicate, we talk; if we don't, chances are we won't be living with them much longer.

How many anguished nights have John and I

spent, clinging by our toenails to the separate edges of our double bed because we have had a tiff and are "not speaking!"

One ghastly night I ended up on the living room couch. John insisted that the bed was the sanctification of our marriage, and come injured feelings, harsh words, or whatever—we belonged there. He would not budge, which I thought was very ungentlemanly, so I did. It was rotten. I didn't sleep a wink that night.

We now have a new rule in our family relations— all differences are to be talked through before we go to bed. Of course, that sometimes means that we are still hassling, come 2 A.M., and sheer emotional exhaustion leads us to reconciliation, which is probably God's way of saying, "Make it up, you two!"

When it comes to talking, God's line is never busy and he will never hang up on us. He will never say, "Can't you wait till half time!" He will not scowl and grouch, "Heavens, woman, it is third down on the five yard line with only 37 seconds left in the game and the score tied!"

He is always available, waiting as anxiously as a courting lover, to hear our voice . . . we call it prayer.

When we live with someone, we eat and we drink with them. No matter how much we talk, if we don't eat we will starve to death.

I feast on the word of God—it has no calories and is full of energy. The scriptures are my stress tabs for the day, and I wear the garment of praise—it is always in style.

In my purse I carry around a little blue booklet

called *The Bible When You Want It.* It is small and flat and has indexed scriptures under the headings, "doubt, loneliness, sorrow, fear, illness, anger, joy, love, confidence," and many more.

When I need a shot of spiritual adrenalin I flip to the relative heading and read such comforting words as, "The Lord is the strength of my life, why should I be afraid?" (Psalm 27:1).

One of the most challenging is, "Ye have not because ye ask not." I don't want to get to heaven, face my Lord, and have Him say, "But Fay . . . you never asked me for that!"

I ask for joy.

For the fullness of all that Jesus is to radiate in and through all that I can become in him. Then I practice my joy. Practice makes perfect.

When Ian was ten, he came whistling into the kitchen one day, threw his school books down on the counter, and said, "Hey Mom, can I practice my kissing on you?"

Reeling with astonishment, I said, "Certainly not! And furthermore, I don't want you practicing your kissing on anyone."

But the boy had a point. He was not about to venture forth into the scarey world of girls an inexperienced kisser.

I can remember my first kiss—I could have used some practice!

The kids have tacked up on my refrigerator door: "Be happy, or shut up!" Most times we can deliberately choose to develop a cheerful disposition.

During a tour through Europe an evangelist and

his young aide registered at a hotel after a heavy day of meetings. Late that night as they were getting ready for bed, the young man heard gales of laughter coming from the evangelist's adjoining room.

"Oh," he thought, "the preacher must have visitors."

The laughter continued and his curiosity got the better of him. Determined not to be left out of the fun, he pulled on a robe and knocked on the door.

The evangelist opened it, dressed in his pajamas.

"Yes?" he asked.

"Have you got company?" asked the young man, "I heard laughter and I thought I'd come over."

"Ha-ha," chuckled the evangelist, "what you heard was me. Every night, the last thing before I turn in, I practice my laughing. Then I practice it again first thing in the morning. It shakes up my liver and keeps me fit."

Norman Cousins says much the same thing and he has written *Anatomy of an Illness* to prove his point. While critically ill, Cousins found, "If I watched Marx Brothers movies and had ten minutes of solid laughter, I could have a night of pain free sleep without any medication. Humor provides the essential vitamin of the soul."

He made the correlation that if negative emotions such as fear, pain, stress, suppressed rage, and hate cause secretions in the brain to dry up so that it cannot do its job well, then the positive emotions of faith, hope, love, laughter, and the will to live must have a role in the stimulation of those secretions.

"The tragedy of life is not death but what dies inside us while we live," he says. "We can be programmed to live, or programmed to die."

My husband and I decided to practice our laughter for one week. Last thing at night and first thing in the morning, we would sit bolt upright in bed and force ourselves to roar with laughter. Once we started we did not have to force—the sheer absurdity took over and we could not stop.

You never saw two children come running into a bedroom so fast! We had a whale of a good time, and it did shake up our livers and make us feel fit, but our children nearly had nervous breakdowns!

Like the Confederate soldier who asked for "all things" that he might enjoy life, but instead was "given life" that he might enjoy all things—we take life and enjoy it.

Now I leap out of bed in the morning with the joy of the Lord as my promise and my strength. I rush to the bathroom mirror and make eye contact, not with the phantom pallor I see reflected there, but with God the Father, God the Son, and God the Holy Spirit living in and through the commitment of my life, and I say, "Good morning, Lord, what have you got planned for us today?"

William Carey tells us, "Expect great things from God—attempt great things for God."

When our get up and go has got up and gone, *his* get up and go will give us a shove!

Passing Through the Middle Ages

I know exactly when it happened. The very moment I stepped out of the fountain of youth and plunged, bottoms-up, into the murky waters of middle age.

The scenario seems fitting.

The crimson and gold trappings of the Pasadena Huntington-Sheraton Hotel have a turn-of-the-century elegance, conjuring up an era when the clatter of dapple-greys pulled flower-bedecked buggies through the portico of its long circular driveway. Ivy vines, digging roots of memory through cracks in a stone foundation, rise thick tentacles to cling around the beams of a covered wooden promenade. The boards creak underfoot and tell of lovers' knots tied in the magic of its filtered moonlight.

Through the midnight hours, bridal suites whisper secrets in the walls and the sweet murmurs of ecstasy trap in echo chambers drifting down the halls. In its massive ballroom ghosts of frolics past, dressed in long flowing chiffon and pearls, tails and white silk ties, pop champagne corks and dance, mingling with the spiked heels and short swaying fringes that shimmy to the music of the Boopity-Boop girl.

Moods and tempos change, but through the decades the Huntington-Sheraton sparkles consistently as one of the brightest jewels in the crown city of Pasadena.

As snowflakes twirl the first breath of winter, and most of the nation digs in for a deep freeze, the California sun breaks morning rays across its sweeping lawns to set the dew on fire. Here, at the poolside patio, for many years the Tournament of Roses chose its royal court. Studied grace and fluttering hearts glided many a young girl's hopes and dreams past the fancy of the judges on the reviewing stand.

In 1927 Francesca Falk Miller caught the magic of the moments:

> Oh the crimson of each sunset
> And the glowing pink of dawn,
> Royal colors of the roses
> Holding court upon the lawn.
> Oh the joy, the smiles, the fragrance
> Of a land that knows no gloom,
> Just a peaceful sun-kissed heaven
> When the roses are in bloom.

With each New Year comes a bustling crowd to trample the lush carpets. Pleasure and ambition mull with romance and excitement—they bubble in and focus on the parade of all parades . . . Mary Pickford, Charlie McCarthy and Edgar Bergen, Shirley Temple, Bob Hope, and Billy Graham have all participated in the overnight celebrations preliminary to leading the way as Grand Marshals to the granddaddy of the football games—the Rose Bowl.

There traditions of Stanford, Notre Dame, Michigan, Alabama, USC thunder over the turf. The crowd roars as statistics tumble. Wrong-way Riegels, running the ball back to his own one yard line in a turnabout that still dumbfounds sports history; the upsets in the last few seconds of play—they liven up the archives of the Huntington-Sheraton Hotel.

Sitting at my desk in the main lobby, I looked out on a tranquil scene. A white lattice gazebo joined a horseshoe of flowers. Poppies and snapdragons spaced with clumps of yellow daisies garnished the rose garden with a rainbow of brilliant color.

It seemed innocent enough. I was filling in for a friend who had established a relocation service, networking through major hotels in the United States. I was a point of information and hospitality, and was to exude a warm charm that would win goodwill and influence clients in the direction of our major accounts.

Under the glass across the front of my desk was a map detailing the complex freeway system that joins the cities of Southern California—always a web of confusion to the visiting motorist. A small rack held complimentary copies, stamped with our logo, and available "For Your Convenience."

He was from the *Paris Match*. Debonair, taller than the average Frenchman, with cornflower-blue eyes that burst springtime through dark, long lashes.

There was purpose in his stride. Pausing just long enough to light up a fresh cigarette, he nodded a quick greeting and bent over the map on my desk.

Thinking that I could better assist him by reading directions right-side-up, I walked around and cheerily smiled, "Can I help you?"

He straightened, took a short deliberate step backward, and inhaled. He looked first at my ankles, then spiraled a slow, discriminatory gaze, like a barley twist, around my legs, up past my hips and waist, to linger for a moment at my bust. He burned a tantalizing second on my lips, circled my hair, then, in a moment of poignant truth, those springtime eyes met mine and turned to winter.

He flicked the ash from his cigarette onto the crimson carpet, and said abruptly, "No."

Taking a "For Your Convenience" map from the rack, he spun on his heel and walked off.

I was left standing in the aftershock of faded glory.

One word, casually tossed, intersected the complacency of my status quo.

It was not a "No–!" nor a "No–?" Not even a "No ..." which may have held the tinge of regret. The finality of his "No" period was match point from *Paris Match!*

He had found a nerve ending, like the elusive tip on a spool of thread, and unraveled me. I crumpled in a tangled heap, fuming with a combination of rage, insult, hurt, rejection, and the awful realization that I was no longer stimuli to a man's libido.

I had grown up with the hubba-hubba generation, when long loud wolf whistles were not considered sexual harassment, but a compliment to a well-turned curve. I would blush, or scowl in mock annoyance, but secretly I was very pleased that I had what it took to get "the look."

My face fell like a mudslide. I sat down hard and bit my bottom lip.

I doodled a picture of Marie Antoinette getting her head chopped off by Robespierre. Then I thought of Napoleon and the Duke of Wellington at the Battle of Waterloo, and I gloated, "Jolly good— one for our side!"

I made up my mind to thoroughly dislike the French with their can-can girls, Folies Bergere, escargot, and naughty thoughts. But then I remembered bon ami, bon appetit, Pouilly-Fuisse, deja vu, the lilting delight of Maurice Chevalier, and blossoms on the Champs-Elysees. These smoothed out the creases on my psyche and I had to love them in spite of my encounter with their gauche journalist. When I had mustered up enough courage I went sniveling into the ladies lounge to confront my image in the long mirror.

(Some years ago I visited Garden Grove Community Church. The Crystal Cathedral was still under construction, but even then the church was an impressive structure. I used a rest room in the Sunday School building. Whether or not it was part of Robert Schuller's projection of "possibility thinking" I don't know, but in that rest room—and maybe even in all his rest rooms, men's included, which would be a good idea—was a mirror that made one look slimmer and taller. Never have I spent so much time twirling and swirling, "oohing" and "ahhing."

Afraid that I had slid down the drain, my companion came looking for me. She caught her reflection in that mirror, and Garden Grove had captivated one more recruit.

Forget the theology, forget the impact of the preaching, forget the voices of heavenly choirs, the television program, the chandelier elegance of glittering glass . . . ditch the church growth programs and outreach ministries, all we need are possibility mirrors throughout our facilities to double, triple, or even quadruple attendance each Sunday. Add glasses of cranberry juice, served during the coffee hour, and the flood tide of the flush will pull people to the reflected regeneration of their new image of loveliness that will immediately sign them up on the roster of church membership!

Those mirrors should be mandatory—everywhere.)

As it was, the image I confronted was ten pounds overweight, the gathered skirt of my pastel sun dress was not only not flattering, it made me look like a barrel, and I noticed flab on my underarms.

I burst into tears!

The elixir of youth is spelled THIN.

When I was carrying our first baby, my husband put his arms around me and said, "Well honey, your anchor's dragging, and your cargo's shifting, but you're still my dream boat!"

Eighteen years later I was no longer with child, but my anchor was still dragging and my cargo was still shifting—I had entered middle age.

There is a navigational term called "midcourse correction." This is a point on the chart when directions need checking, the compass needs verifying, and adjustments need to be made in order to maintain a "steady as she goes," or the ship may flounder on a very unsteady course.

My ship was floundering and it was time, long overdue, for a series of midcourse corrections.

I ran home and smeared egg white all over my face. Every wrinkle disappeared. I looked twenty years younger, only better.

"Quick," I shouted, "somebody take my picture!"

Nobody was there to hear me. Trouble with egg white is that it is effective for only twenty minutes at a time.

That night I faced the family. I had a triangular "frown-eraser" plaster in between my eyes, and Elastin cream coating my face and neck. Porcelana glistened on the age spots on my hands.

"Holy baloney!" said my son when he saw me.

"I am tired of looking like a frump," I said.

"So, what else is new?" he sniped.

"You can't talk about my wife that way!" said my husband.

"Aw . . . Mom!" said my daughter as she gave me a hug.

"Now hear this," I continued. "Our bodies are being destroyed by inertia. I think we should join a health spa."

"Right on!" said my son, his eyes lighting up. "Let's go to one with all the machines."

"Aw . . . Mom!" said my daughter.

"How much will it cost?" said my husband suspiciously.

That Christmas I gave John a membership to the local spa, with me tacked on as a rider at a specially reduced rate. The children could come once in a while as guests, but on our pinched budget they would have to wait for full-fledged membership until they could help pay their own way.

"It's a bummer," said my son.

"Aw . . . Mom!" said my daughter.

"Men and women mixed?" asked my husband, picking up an astonishing enthusiasm as he sucked in his stomach. "Or men and women separate?"

Straightening to my full height (5'1"), I took a short step backward, and inhaled (my breath only, as at an early age I decided hot fudge sundaes were a lot tastier than cigarettes). I looked first at his ankles (those French have their priorities right), then I deliberately spiraled a slow, discriminatory gaze, like a barley twist, around his legs, up past his bulging torso, until my eyes met his in a moment of poignant truth . . .

"No." I said.

"For the sake of the women, dahling," I explained, "better make it men and women, separate."

He let his tummy pop out and said, "Rats!"

My daughter waved in front of me a magazine ad for a digital computer scale. "Here, this is what we need," she said.

It claimed an electronic breakthrough that would:

"Memorize your weight and the weights of three other family members, so you can compare previous weights with present weights to keep fit, look good, feel healthy."

"Yeah," I groaned, "just what we need . . . to have every Tom, Dick, and Harry or Sally, Jill, and Jane that comes into this house and uses the bathroom pushing my own personalized 'Individual Memory Assignment Button.' Then have my past weight compared with my present weight flashed in red on the digital display readout! When high technology starts publicizing my vital statistics, it has gone too far! Next thing we know, they will add a synthesizer audio circuit that will give us a computerized voice tittering, 'Ha-ha-ha, Mrs. Angus, you cheated on your diet this week—naughty, naughty . . . three pounds gained!' "

I pulled on the black leotard and tights from my ballet days. Every bump of cellulite showed. Years back, I remembered looking at my mother's figure slowly changing and thinking, "My bottom is *never* going to look like that!"

My bottom looked exactly like that.

It was hard to believe that at one time I had every muscle ramrod tight and under disciplined control. It was harder to believe I had ever had any muscle at all.

For the sake of propriety I added a cover-up sweatshirt. All in all, thanks to my legs which were still pretty good, I looked quite professional.

Early in the new year I presented myself at the

registration desk of the spa. The manager was named Abdul. He had a dark receding hairline, pitch black eyes, and a shiny skin that glistened rippling muscles through the mesh of his workout shirt. He looked down at me and flashed a broad, bright smile.

"Trim n'tone," he said, and he took me over to one of the chrome machines. It was a twentieth-century replica of the medieval rack. Suddenly I felt a camaraderie with the victims of the Spanish Inquisition—an omen of things yet to come.

"Easy warmup," he said, "five minutes bicycle, ten times for each leg on the lifts, ten times for each arm on the weights, here on the slant for the sit-ups, aerobics to oxygenate . . . we get you in shape real good!"

He wrote the program down on my chart, just under the depressing figures of my weight and the measurements of my hips and upper thighs.

A chubby woman with a sweet face came in. I decided that she looked a sympathetic sort, so I sheepishly followed alongside her.

Looks are deceiving.

She was Atilla the Hen, pushing steel and tyrannizing the stress in every mechanical device that confronted us. By comparison, I was Chicken Little with the sky falling in.

"You should have seen me when I first came in," she chortled, lifting thirty pounds with one arm.

My eyes got bigger, my spirits got lower, my body got breathless, and my mind got boggled!

My ship was not only floundering, there was the

strong possibility it would sink from sheer exhaustion in the process, but I was determined to make the midcourse correction in the navigational chart of my physical fitness.

(Wanna see me lift thirty pounds with one arm?)

Satchel Paige said, "How old would you be if you didn't know how old you was?" Twaddle! There comes a time in the biological time clock when a woman's estrogen count and her hot flashes tell her *exactly* how old she is—she's middle-aged, that's how old!

When a man's stress levels blink stop lights through the fast lane of his high blood pressure, and his cholesterol count puts a roadblock in his arteries, he's midlife crisis, that's how old!

Suddenly you find yourself telling the kids, "Go easy on your Dad, he is under a lot of pressure these days, y'know." You tell your husband, "Go easy on the kids, they are going through puberty, y'know." And then, when your back is turned you find that your husband has been telling them, "Go easy on your Mom, she is at that time of life, y'know." Only he does not know how to go easy on her himself and says things like, "For goodness sake, what are you sniffling about now..." or, "Why are all the windows wide open when it's freezing cold in here?" and he slams them shut and turns the furnace up.

One day your twelve-year-old son phones from school and you say, "Hello there, Janet!" which makes him scowl at you for the next two years, or until his voice drops, whichever comes first.

Your daughter has her first broken romance, and cries nonstop for three weeks, refusing to eat. She loses ten pounds in the process while you put on fifteen by eating all her refusals so as not to waste them.

Grandma whispers, "I don't know what to do with your father, he has been retired for only one month, and already he's moping about the house and driving me nuts."

Grandpa gets you in a corner and says, "Your mother sure is edgy these days!"

It all adds up to a huge conspiracy with everyone in the family tippy-toeing around everyone else and smiling knowing smiles at each other, which does not fool anyone, but only aggravates the condition of the people involved.

Welcome to the middle ages!

Although at times we may feel as skittish as we did at seventeen, and at others as senile as we probably will at 117, it is time to admit that at fifty we are not the people we were at twenty-five, which generally speaking is good news.

Passing through the middle ages takes strategic planning and sailing under the flag called *cope*.

It is an opportunity to redefine our values; to intercept our attitudes and analyze our alternatives; to make whatever midcourse corrections are necessary to keep us on an even keel; and to reset our directives for the future.

It is the determination to live on the *forward urge* rather than on the backward skid.

We cannot change the past, but we can learn from

it. We can influence the present, and we can move confidently ahead. Like the soldier who led a charge up a hill with the bullets whizzing around about him—"Come back," yelled his comrades. "I can't come back," he shouted, "you come on!"

With Paul, "forgetting those things which are behind, and reaching forth unto those things which are before," we press on, "toward the mark for the prize of the high calling of God in Christ Jesus" (Philippians 3:13–14).

My husband tends to be a backward-looking person. An avid historian, he sits up in bed with twenty volumes of the works of Washington Irving in his nightstand, and immerses himself in the past.

I, on the other hand, tend to be a futurist. I sit up in bed with the works of Alvin Toffler, Vance Packard, and Isaac Asimov in my nightstand.

Between us, there is a danger of missing the present altogether!

So we make appointments with each other, "I say, do you suppose we could fit in a little romance at 10:15?" (Middle age synchronizes its time clock to the fact that 10 p.m. is tired, 11 p.m. is utterly exhausted!)

He is always willing, and I am always willing, and most times we are early for the appointment, which goes to show that basic urges are far more motivational than backward urges or forward urges.

To keep in touch with the present, middle age makes appointments and writes notes to itself constantly.

"Pay the utility bills," or, "I am parked in D-2 on

the lower level." Or, "My telephone number is
_____."

Ever since a fellow middle-ager passed me a note that said, "If you haven't thought a new thought, read something interesting, or developed a point of view in the last forty-eight hours, check your pulse, you may be dead!" I make appointments with myself to check my pulse regularly, and to take time to think.

I keep a list of "Thoughts Worth Thinking." These are gleaned from what I have been reading, or from a sermon here and there. Occasionally (very) a provocative television program. Sometimes (rare) a clever thought from my husband, and once in a while (startling) one of my own original thoughts, all of which give enormous momentum to my thinking process.

When my mind feels sluggish and dull, I just pull out my "Thoughts Worth Thinking" list and I am immediately plugged into a fascinating conversation with myself.

Considering that psychologists tell us that subconsciously we talk to ourselves at the rate of 1,300 words per minute, the vital question is: what are we saying? What we are saying originates with what we are thinking.

On learning about the list that I keep, well-meaning friends frequently clip and send me things that they think I should be thinking about. I am very cordial and nice, but deep down inside, instead of putting my thinking apparatus on overload, I wish they would think about these things themselves and then tell me what they thought. In the olden days, before television, this used to be called cultivating the art of conversation.

I also keep a list of "Thoughts *Not* Worth Thinking." The Bible calls these "vain imaginations" that should be cast down. I cast them down by writing them down.

Regrets such as, "Why did I say that, when I should have said this . . ." or resentments such as, "Why did he say that, when he could have said this . . ." I index under the headings of mean, nasty, deadly (watch out for those), silly, and utterly useless. After I have written them down, which is a good catharsis for getting them out of my system, I cross them out. They are still there, as documentation of my own time-wasting folly, but negated as thoughts not worth thinking.

When my not worth thinking list gets longer than my worth thinking list, I realize that I am on the backward skid rather than on the *forward urge*, and it is time for another midcourse correction.

One difficulty is in sorting out what thoughts to place on which list. Such as, what would happen if the *National Enquirer* got a hold of the thoughts I have listed under mean, nasty, deadly, silly, and utterly useless.

My husband checks my lists periodically just to make sure his name does not show up under "Thoughts Not Worth Thinking."

As a precaution, and probably in self-defense, he

purchased a 7 pound, 2,174 page, 1929 edition of the *Lincoln Library of Essential Information*, from a yard sale. It has quizzes behind each of its subject sections and when I get a bit uppity, he throws these at me (the questions, not the 7 pound book, which is fortunate).

"Where and when was the first recorded raising of the American flag over a school?" he asks smugly. "What is the Dawes Plan designed to accomplish— tell how it aims to secure this result. What is the salary of the vice president of the United States?"

It turns out that my intelligence quotient on essential information is sub-zero. This is very intimidating. I live with the apprehension that one day my husband will compile his own list of essential information and that I may not be on it!

What we think about is tremendously important to keep us moving on the *forward urge*.

Statistics tell us that approximately 50 percent of what we worry about never comes to pass. Another 40 percent does not amount to much if and when it does come to pass. And 5 percent we cannot do anything about anyway, which leaves us with a mere 5 percent about which we may have a legitimate reason to worry. Most of our worries belong on our "Thoughts *Not* Worth Thinking" list.

"To think" is the key to staying mentally alive, alert, informed, and involved. In the late 1930s, several great theologians and philosophers were asked to look back in retrospect and choose what specific discipline they would cultivate if they had their youth to live over.

One said, "At the age of ten we wonder, at twenty we imagine, at thirty we cogitate, at forty we think, at fifty we have 'an idea or two,' at sixty we have two ideas, and at seventy we are working on 'one idea.' The sooner you get to that one idea the better." He concluded that he would strive to be an original thinker.

The blasphemy of middle age is, "I can't be bothered!" It clouds our vision, cancels our options, and catapults us down the backward skid.

A few years ago, Gail Sheehy (the author of *Passages*) took a survey through the readers of *Redbook Magazine*. The results were startling. Analyzing the replies of some 52,000 women, from assorted age levels, she found that listed as top priority were the values of "mature love, family security, and inner harmony."

The middle-aged woman, in her mid-fifties or up, was the happiest. These were overcomers!

Earlier than most men, generally at thirty-five or forty, many women face midlife crises. This is not to be confused with the menopause.

She may suddenly see her life as mediocrity, her dreams unrealized or shattered. She may be enduring marital strains or she may be traumatized by a sequence of broken relationships that have fractured her self-worth. She feels as though she has been pulled through a hedge backwards and is emotionally and physically disheveled in the process.

"I am nothing but a zero!" one woman told me. "Marvelous," I said. "Now let's figure out a way to put a one in front of it and you'll become a 10!"

We did, and she may not be quite a 10, but maybe—7½?

The overcomer switches her gears and makes the midcourse corrections necessary to move her in a new direction.

Another woman told me that midlife crisis was the exact time in her life when she came to a conviction of faith. She simply could not endure the thought of death as the final solution to life, and floundered about in search of meaning. The promise of *"everlasting life"* put zest and courage into what had been dismal days.

Sheehy found that by the time she has reached the big 5–0 the mature woman has established a "seasoned" happiness. Such women have, as she puts it, "validated themselves by overcoming dependency on other people's approval and reached a new tolerance and satisfaction with their mates."

She assures us that "each stage ahead holds the promise of a new beginning in which it is possible to throw off old fears and conflicts, leave behind outlived roles and release a more certain, valid self who is capable of loving more richly and living more fiercely."

If only we will bother to do so!

We need to remember the promise, "To him that overcometh will I grant to sit with me in my throne, even as I also overcame and am set down with my Father in his throne . . ." (Revelation 3:21).

Men who most successfully survive passage through the middle ages are those who do not fret and stew about the things not accomplished in their lives, but grab a firm hold on the present, thankful for the simple pleasures of love, laughter, and an honest day's work well done. The affirmation of a support group of friends and family puts the base-line at "having someone who cares whether you come home or not."

The average man has not climbed the pinnacle on the corporate peaks of success, but does that really matter? Many who have may have lost their happiness in the process. Success, as defined by the world's hype, is most often achieved at enormous price, and sometimes with devastating consequence. This does not mean that we shrug off healthy ambition. We are programmed for productivity, and thumb-twiddling inertia leads to hardening of the arteries.

When we moderate the tyranny of the immediate by carefully and prayerfully set priorities, well-cut patterns for living balanced by realistic goals, we crumble the walls of life on the treadmill of the Skinner box. This maintains the thrust of the *forward urge* while eliminating many of the pressure points that lead to the crises in mid life crises.

In the middle of my busiest times, when I am frequently squeezed by the deadlines of commitment, I deliberately pause. I may take a stroll around the garden, cup of tea in hand, and let the pleasure of a hummingbird taking nectar from the orange blossoms expand my soul. Or I may take a walk around the block, even if I am out of town. It is by putting space in the rapid pace of our schedules that our minds are aerated, our thoughts ventilated, and our perspectives validated.

If I am too busy to smell the flowers, then I am *too* busy.

Few of us fulfill the "impossible dream" so blithely handed to us on our high school graduation cards. But there are possible dreams that we can fulfill at any age.

If we feel that life is passing us by, it may be a truism that needs dealing with. For many, life *is* passing them by. Daily we are handed a blank check that many of us never bother to fill in and cash.

On terminating a rollercoaster marriage that bumped its way through plummeting *downs* that never did pull *up*, a friend of mine said, "Now, I can travel and do some of the things I have always dreamed of doing."

It made me think. Was I being a hinderance to John in anything that he earnestly wanted to do in his lifetime? God forbid!

He was the facilitator of our family. Hardworking, sometimes to extremes—concerned and caring about our happiness—had we ever thought about the possibility of the family facilitating his heart's desire?

That night I suggested a long walk.

Rousseau said that he needed bodily motion to set his soul vibrating and give audacity to his thoughts. I have found walking good therapy to clear the cobwebs from the mind. Besides, one meets all sorts of interesting people on walks. People walking with people, people walking with dogs, people walking without dogs, and dogs walking without people.

The cadence of my short staccato step against his long stride broke a rhythm into the sporadic twitter of birds bedding down for the night. My hand held tightly onto his.

"Is there anything at all that you have really wanted to do in your life, like visit some place that you've always wanted to see, that you can't because of your responsibilities to me and the kids?" I asked.

"W-e-l-l," he said with a sly grin. "I guess there's always Bo Derek . . ."

"Seriously!" I insisted.

After a mile or two, probably concerned that I would refuse to turn about and retrace the route home until he shared his heart's desire, he confessed that he had always had a yen to visit Yugoslavia.

"It's said to be a beautiful country," he explained, "with its coastline on the Adriatic Sea. It's in Belgrade where the Sava River joins the Danube."

He could have knocked me over with a feather! Our roots in Scotland or Ireland, yes, but never in my wildest imagination would I have thought of Yugoslavia—I can hardly spell it, much less speak it!

"W-e-l-l," I stuttered, somewhat shaken, "let's go."

"You crazy or something?" he said. "With two kids in college and tuition costs rising?"

"Darling," I said, "I don't care if we have to sell all the furniture and mortgage the mortgage—you and I are going to Yugoslavia."

"When?" he teased.

"Before we hit our dotage, that's for sure!"

Some months back we had met an elderly couple at a business dinner. They had just returned from a trip to Europe.

"Go now, pay later, if you have to," they advised.

They had scrimped and saved for most of their lives, and then by the time they had enough money for their dream trip, they were not well enough to enjoy it.

So far the money has not come in, but the atlas has come out. We are setting Yugoslavia as a possible dream, and we are moving ahead on the *forward urge*, determined to get there.

When we are ninety-four, I want us to be able to smile at each other and say, "Hey—we made it to Yugoslavia!"

Knowing my husband, he will wink and say, "I've been thinking about Nicaragua . . ."

Grief Is a Love Word

When it comes to death, up until quite recently, I considered myself to be unflappable.

After all, I told myself, death should not be thought of as the last sleep, but rather as the last and final awakening—the laurel leaf in the crown of faith.

That is, until quite recently.

Recently, I discovered that when it comes to death—the fact—I am unflappable, but when it comes to dying—the act—I am more than flappable.

With all my spiritualizing, with all my theorizing, with all the platitudes, filed carefully through the years; with all my emotions neatly tagged and compartmentalized, with all my prerogatives and precautions analytically processed.... Silly me, I had not reckoned on the sting of hurt that peels them away like leaves on an artichoke, nibbled one by one, until all that is exposed is the heart, vulnerable, ready to be stripped and devoured.

I had not reckoned *grief.*

Grief is a love word. We do not grieve for those we do not love.

To love is to risk losing, but not to love is to have already lost. So we love, we lose, and we grieve.

We grieve not only for those we love and lose in death, but for those we love and lose who are not dead.

We grieve for things that could have been but aren't, and things that are but should not be.

Grief can be the friend who walks us through the sorrow and reaches for the joy that seeks us through the pain, or the enemy who stalks us in the shadows, and turns us from the promise of another day.

There is no quick fix for grief. It takes a working through. It sets its own pace and it will not be hurried; what is fast for one is slow for another. For those who grieve, time is not measured by minutes ticking off the hours, days and weeks, but by the counterpoint of heartache against heartease.

Alfred Lord Tennyson's childhood was so tragic and filled with such intense suffering that frequently as a young boy he would run into the churchyard and fling himself on the gravestones, longing for death.

The great joy of his life was his friendship with a college chum—a charming, brilliant, popular student at Cambridge, whom many scholars considered to be one of the finest and most gifted spirits of their day.

When that friend died, too young and too soon, he felt that all that was left for him was to curse God and die. Instead he "worked" his grief.

Tennyson moved the confusion, the pain, and the torturing sorrow of his loss, through hours of grief. Our legacy is *In Memoriam,* from which these stanzas are taken:

Forgive my grief for one removed,
  Thy creature, whom I found so fair,
  I trust he lives in Thee, and there
I find him worthier to be loved . . .

I sometimes hold it half a sin
  To put in words the grief I feel,
  For words, like Nature, half reveal
And half conceal the Soul within . . .

We had been through the war together, she and I.

There was many a day that she saw the hunger hollowing out my eyes, and she gave me her ration of a slice of bread. She patted me to sleep, singing quietly the songs we loved, "When Irish Eyes Are Smiling," "Peggy O'Neil," or "Alice Blue Gown."

Once in a while I would ask for the jolly upbeat of "McNamara's Band"—it took my mind off the cracked chilblains, the festering pussfilled sores on the knuckles of my hands and feet, and the cold that put nausea into the gnawing fear wrapped around my night.

As we shared a cramped corner in a dormitory with sixty-four other women, every blink of an eye, sniffle or sneeze, was amplified and hushed! I would sit bolt upright on my cot, like the prong of a comb broken to bend the wrong way, and study the sleeping figures, flat on their backs around me. They were cut from patterns of life ranging from the cream of the aristocracy to those of "questionable repute!"

Suddenly I would realize that other eyes were probably studying me, and I would slip back between the covers and pull them over my head like a shroud, a confused and frightened little girl.

More than many other things, our two and a half years of internment under the Japanese occupation of China taught us the value of privacy.

Mother wanted to live alone.

She had a tiny cottage not far from where we live in the hills of Sierra Madre. She planted an "English" garden, filled with larkspurs, hollyhocks, sweet William, and huge red and gold dahlias.

"Do come over," she would say, "they are bigger and better than ever this year!"

She said that every year, and indeed, they always seemed bigger and better than ever.

She dug beds of roses and bordered them with pansies, Johnny-jump-ups, and violets.

"Don't pick, just look!" she scolded the children as they passed on their way to school. For the tiny tots, she would go over and over the names of all the shrubs and flowers, as they pointed chubby little fingers and asked endlessly, "What's dat? And dat?"

She taught our own toddlers how to press leaves and flowers in waxed paper, between the pages of a "good fat book." She gave them slips of this and that in tiny pots and sent them home with dirt crusted deep underneath their fingernails.

"Mercy!" I would grumble, "I'll never get this clean."

The sirens screamed one morning. The paramedics called.

They had found her lying on her kitchen floor. The heart attack had come in predawn hours. Her bright copper tea kettle was topsy-turvy in the sink where she had dropped it, getting ready for a "wee drop" to woo the morning light.

"Will she pull through?" I asked the doctor.

Grim lines tightened grey around the corners of his mouth.

"He looks so tired," I thought, and I wondered how many sirens had screamed at him through that night.

His hand squeezed mine . . .

"Then teach me how to help her die," I whispered through a throat gone dry, and eyes swimming in a blur of tears.

Thank God for tears.

Our body needs our tears as much as our emotions need to have them flow. They lubricate our eyes and keep them moist; they cleanse and lift a piece of lint, or speck of dust; they wash away the fumes that smart and irritate.

Within each of us are reservoirs brim-full with tears.

Tears of joy and gratitude. Sentimental tears that well up when our hearts are touched—a petal hung with dew, the soft curve of a baby's cheek, or weepy, inexplicable tears that flow with a lovely piece of music.

Tears of frustration and anger. Tears of disappointment and hurt. Tears of regret. Then the sobbing, choking tears of grief.

Thank God for men strong enough to cry.

One man said, "Sometimes it's just not enough to

shake another man's hand firmly, look him in the eye, and nod. Sometimes it's not enough to put your arm around a woman, and pat her gently on the back while she cries for both of you."

Jesus wept—thank God.

The irregular bleep of the monitoring machine etched crazy patterns up and down the screen. Labored breathing beat the tempo, like a metronome, pacing a litany of benediction that made the bed an altar . . .

Inhale—Lord have mercy!
Exhale—Christ have mercy!
Inhale—Lord have mercy!

Grief squeezed me so that every bone felt crushed and words jumbled, inarticulate.

The cymbidium orchid grows from ugly bulbs and it sprouts plain tapered leaves. It does not bloom unless it is very tightly squeezed, clustered in a pot.

Once I put a cymbidium clump into the ground, thinking it needed space to stretch. It never flowered. It is only when squeezed almost to death that the matchless beauty of its stem buds six, seven, sometimes as many as eight pale, exquisite flowers . . . and under each a drop of honey-sweet nectar forms.

"So plant me in the soil of your strength, O Lord," I prayed. "Squeeze the grief in me, and from the ugly root of pain and sorrow grow something beautiful to bloom in joy."

Consecrated grief bears its own unique eternal bloom, and tears, like nectar, drop honey-sweet to God.

I sat for hours and rubbed circulation into ice cold feet. Just days before they had tingled on a freshly watered lawn. I tried to smooth away the bursts of blue and red veins that broke against the swelling skin.

I brushed hair damp with the struggle to survive, and spread lotion over lips parched dry. I quietly sang the songs we loved—those lilting Irish melodies. I patted her, as she had patted me, to ease the gnawing fear now wrapped around her night.

And when my prayers dried up, and my heart shriveled with denial, I read the Lamentations.

"The compassions of the Lord fail not, therefore have I hope."

I said them, like a rosary:

"It is of the Lord's mercies that we are not consumed . . . *because His compassions fail not*."

"They are new every morning; great is God's faithfulness . . . *because His compassions fail not*."

"The Lord is my portion says my soul; therefore I will hope in Him . . . *because His compassions fail not*."

"The Lord is good to them that wait for Him, to the soul that seeks Him . . . *because His compassions fail not*."

"The Lord drew near to me in the day that I called upon Him; he said, Fear not . . . *because His compassions fail not*."

"O Lord, you have pleaded the causes of my soul; you have redeemed my life . . . because Your compassions fail not!"

Through those crucial weeks, I sat by my mother's

bed and stroked a thousand memories. They clogged my mind, and stumbled over each other pushing for recall.

I relived childhood adventures and told her stories of "remember when. . . ."

Tsingtao in the summer time. Enormous waves that tossed us up like corks. Tiger lilies growing wild along the cliffs and donkey rides trotting down the beach. I gave her visual images to conjure up familiar things and trip a switch to bring her back to consciousness.

I named the family names, and tasted once again our Chinese dinners at Sun Ya's with shark's fin soup, Peking duck, and the wailing music of the Sing-Song girls.

The angry words that clawed our past—resentments boiling hot, and ugly, ugly things. They all turned bittersweet, *because the compassions of the Lord fail not!*

She was a little sparrow, fallen, lying on her back with legs pulled up and eyes shut tight against the light. Jesus saw this sparrow fall—so did I. He threw his mantle over us and covered with his love, we warmed, and melted icy, ugly things.

I told her that I loved her, and I wondered if she heard.

The children didn't want to come.

We had nursed so many small furry creatures, swaddled in strips of towel, or cuddled in our arms, trying to tease life back into lifeless little bodies. Hamsters, rabbits, rats, kittens, dogs and guinea pigs too numerous to count.

From the time he was five, my son had learned to dig small graves, deep around the roots of the old oak tree in the upper terrace. There we committed back to the earth pets who had joyed and comforted our lives. We placed small rings of stones to mark the spots.

My daughter and I wept bitter tears the night we forgot to latch the coop and our hens fell prey to racoons. As one huddled, mortally wounded, we bent to our knees and stroked her ruffled feathers, "Oh Hilda, we're so sorry!" She peeped a pathetic little peep, as though to give us absolution, then keeled over—the next day she was dead.

Cha-Cha lapped up antifreeze. "So sweet, so good," she thought in her own doggy way, and one more friend returned as dust to dust.

The children came.

They learned the language of goodbye: the tender care that sits and holds a hand gone limp. They wet a cloth and wiped my Mother's brow and wet her lips with lemon swabs.

I thought about another swab—a sponge with vinegar . . . a hill called Golgotha and a mother standing there.

She could not reach to brush his hair, or stroke his hand—his hands were nailed to a cross. She could not put her mother's tender touch to wipe his brow.

She could not "work" her grief with acts of love. She stood and watched the blood and water flowing down. Her heart was squeezed to simply being there.

I wondered if a thousand memories clogged her mind. If thoughts went back to the babe in swaddling clothes, the visit to the Temple. I wondered if, standing there, she remembered, "I must be about my Father's business," and water changed to wine.

When he looked down at her . . . I wondered if the burden of her grief pierced a dagger through his heart more than the soldier's spear; and if to see the agony reflected in her eyes caused him pain far greater than the nails and crown of thorns.

The friends who stood with her to watch and wait. . . . For those who can do nothing but stand and watch and wait, their grief is caught for all eternity in the cluster at the cross!

For nights I lay across my mother's bed and pushed my body warmth against her legs, so she would know I was still there.

Days and nights mixed up and time stood still, until the mystery of that moment—the sun rose in my heart . . . my mother looked at me and smiled.

One day she won't, and I will burst my reservoir of tears.

My grief observed became my grief renewed.

How many weeks of intensive care spaced themselves through the years?

Life clung to life with tenacious arrogance. Brittle bones broke on brittle bones, fibrillations fluttered an already weakened heart and minor strokes frightened both of us. We called her our "resurrection lady." She bounced in and out of hospital like a yo-yo—I would put her in the arms of Jesus, convinced this was the end, and he would touch, then turn her back to me!

She was moved to the facilities of extended care.

Up and down the corridors, three by three, like wide-eyed pigeons tucked into roosts, small grey faces tufted with white peered out at me. They cooed little moans, or screamed at the predators of their night, waiting for those who never came.

A grief renewed for those who did not care. Poorer than the poor, they simply were not there.

Wheeled about in chairs, like gaily colored parakeets splashing red and green, or sunshine yellow plumage in their floral smocks, eager heads nodded acquiescence and dull eyes lit up to a word of kindness.

One man caught my arm each day, "Don't let me down," he begged, "please don't let me down!" I wondered how many people had let him down and dashed his hopes against a stoic silence.

A grief renewed for life, distilled to the essence of water sipped through a straw in a paper cup, a box of tissue, and the lifeline of a catheter processing its steady drip beside the bed.

The stored-up knowledge of the years translated to the intense concentration of stuttering to string together a simple sentence.

"Prophecies shall fail; tongues shall cease; knowledge shall vanish—love never fails" (1 Corinthians 13:8).

Love remained.

Strangers dressed in white became mother, father, child, and friend to those who had no mother, father, child or friend.

It fairly burst my heart! "Lord use your love flowing through my heart to be a rainbow, shining through their rain," I prayed. Once again I consecrated grief, and suddenly with my mother I had many other mothers and fathers up and down the hall.

A chocolate-covered mint, wafer-thin to freshen up a tired, tasteless mouth . . . . As eagerly as postulants, kneeling at a rail, they received a tender mercy. "This, too, we do in remembrance of you."

"My mother died so suddenly," Millie said, "I did not have the opportunity of caring and stroking from her the final pulse of life. But I determined to use my grief to do it for someone else." She does. Twice a week, and leaves her kiss, printed pale pink on each brow.

The griefs of guilt and regret are those with which we punish ourselves.

"If only I had . . ." or, "If only I hadn't . . ."

They flagellate our consciences and swill us in the limbo of our anxieties. These need a healing of our memories to move us out beyond circumstances over which we now have no control, and into affirmation of the present, over which we have a great deal of control. "What is, and what can be," rather than "what was."

Even as love initiates action, grief initiates action.

Her name was Sue.

She was a golden California girl. Blond hair bleached almost platinum by a scorching summer sun, her hazel eyes smoked blue in morning mists, green while surfing through the waves, and by candlelight flecked brown with the warmth of many autumn hues.

She was flippant, bursting with independence, anxious to stretch herself through the vulnerabilities of campus life, and yet a quiver, feather light, that wafted high or low, fanned by the breezes of self-doubt.

They had spent the evening tasting tea. Chamomile, Morning Thunder, Dynasty Green, and the Mixed Herbs of Sleepytime—but it was after midnight and they still were not sleepy.

The new semester had thrown them together; roommates in the hallowed halls of learning. After weeks of explosive tempers and seemingly endless hassles, they were modifying to each other and starting to build a mutual trust.

Lessons in learning were not as hard as lessons in living, or . . . lessons in loving!

Chris scanned the angles of the room, books were everywhere. Her eye sorted through the familiar clutter. Suddenly she saw it. Balanced precariously at the end of a shelf, like a sentry standing at attention, was an empty coke bottle. A slip of white, stained paper curled inside.

She stood and reached, "Hey, Sue, what's this?"

Sue barely raised her eyes. She turned and turned the small square box of tea. She gave a nervous little laugh. Sometimes we laugh because it hurts too much to cry.

Chris lifted the bottle towards the light, "September 22 . . . something pretty special, eh?"

The date lashed open wounds of memory. Sue bit her lip and with her knuckles clenching white, she crushed the paper box.

"That's all he bought me, one lousy bottle of coke!" The words scraped raw against each other— they had a bitter edge.

"I will never, ever forget . . . I sold my virginity for a bottle of coke."

She had carried the grief of her regret for over a year. Not only that, she had raised a monument to it. She put it on display to taunt and mock her. The empty coke bottle with its crumpled date jeered, "*I will never let you forget!*

"A good friend multiplies joy and divides grief," there are times of anguish when others help us to do that which we cannot, or will not do alone.

"One broken dream is not the end of dreaming," wrote Edgar A. Guest. Heaven reached down to Sue that night. With the help of Chris, she turned her grief over to the loving kindness of a God whose *compassions fail not*, and she made peace with herself. A moment's indiscretion that had destroyed her dreams of a love-fulfilled sexuality, rather than a one-night stand, had grown in her a bitter fruit from a bitter root. It could have colored relationships throughout her life. She dug it up and tossed it out.

Taking the empty coke bottle, the girls went outside. Under the stars, winking through palm fronds that etched a tapestry against the sky, they smashed it on a rock. It broke into a hundred pieces, glistening at their feet, and the soiled slip of paper was trodden underfoot.

Arm in arm they turned and walked from the night towards the new beginnings of another day.

Between the hours of two and three o'clock in the morning the body is at its lowest ebb, it is in its most vulnerable state.

For those who grieve for one they love who is not dead, life is suspended in a perpetual state of three o'clock in the morning.

That person might be living right beside us, and grief tugs at our heart for all the things we wish could be, but aren't.

Worse than the rejection of open hostility is the rejection coming through our intimacies. We yearn to reach out and hold and touch, to stroke and love. Instead, we find a wall of indifference and resistance that drowns us in the grief of shut-out love; the hurt of trying to be happy *in spite* of those we love instead of *because of* those we love.

If that one we love has left, we wake through many restless nights, remembering all that used to be. We wonder if they ever stir to think of us, or if in their hearts we are past remembering, while in our hearts they are past forgetting.

There is the grief of "letting go," to watch a child make his own seemingly irreversible mistakes. We fret over all the possibilities, and all the impossibilities. Whether they are well or ill; in pain or trouble;

out of money or in need of help .... We carry them, piggy-back on our prayers, out of sight, and strain like a tortoise looking up over his shell to see their faces.

"Faith is the bird that sings to greet the dawn while it is still dark."

If we take that Indian proverb, and through the dark night of our soul learn to sing its song of faith, we break the pain of heartache and stir the promise of the morning light.

Successful grief recognizes and is not reluctant to "feel" its varied agonies. It balks at all the old familiar places, winces at nostalgic scents, and lingers over mementos.

It gropes with aching arms, inching through the desolation, and moves towards the discovery of the reconstructed life.

I wrote a letter of consolation to a friend whose sister had recently died.

"I find myself laying cards and notes aside," she wrote back, "thinking, 'I'll send these down to Ann—she will love them,' and then stark reality hits, and I realize that I cannot call her on the phone, nor write to her. But then the blessed Holy Spirit reminds me that there is one thing I can still do with her, and that is to *praise God!*"

"The words of the Doxology, 'Praise Him all creatures here below, praise Him above ye heavenly host . . .' have new meaning as I realize that when we praise God we are united with those already with him, and we will all be praising him for eternity!"

Successful grief plants jonquils in the winter sea-

son of the heart and waits to see them burst to life
with reassurance of the spring.

While successful grief does not deny or squelch itself, it does not hold itself hostage to love with the
fear that to stop grieving might mean to stop loving.
It does not stalk and haunt the past, captive in despair, but while treasuring the memories of yesterday, it looks to every new tomorrow as the promise
of another day.

The essentials of the reconstructed life are something to do, something to hope for, and someone to
love.

Parents who suffered the heart-tearing loss of a
child formed a support group called Compassionate
Friends. Knit together by an experience that can
uniquely say, "I understand," they meet and talk
through the hurts of their grief, then they reach out
to others, perhaps in the middle of heartbreak, and
offer themselves as a listening and a leaning post, to
comfort and encourage.

Several years ago seven employees in a large Pasadena hospital met together and shared their mutual
grief in the loss of their mates. "Half of me was
gone," one said. "I felt as though I was seeing life
through only one eye, and hopping on only one foot.
My balance was out of whack!"

They decided to meet monthly to reinforce and
encourage one another and to simply ease the loneliness by doing things together—to balance one another.

They call themselves *Patchwork*. I like the name.
Patchwork takes the remnants of many pieces (our

broken hearts), many colors (our varied experiences), and many different textures (our individual person-alities), and stitches them all together in a brilliant and beautiful design, unattainable through any other means. In the same way, we patch and reconstruct our lives.

Each summer our family goes fishing in the high Sierras of California. I wait all year to feel that tug of trout on the end of my line, and I drool over the thought of a fish fry in the great outdoors.

How good it is to get away from the smog, the pressure points of the time zones in our lives, and to renew ourselves in the clear, crisp air of lakes, streams, and high plateaus. The Chinese call it the pause that lets the soul catch up with the body.

One of our traditions is to take the gondola ride up to the top of Mammoth mountain. The panorama is breathtaking. It is the top of the world—one step away from heaven.

But . . . for all its beauty, nothing grows on the top of Mammoth mountain. Fruit grows in the valley.

If we lived only on the mountain tops of life, our souls would be barren. It is in the deep and low places, often in the places hidden from everyone but God; it is in the valleys of our sorrows and our griefs that we cultivate . . . understanding, compassion, courage, sensitivity, sympathy, kindness, and all those tender mercies that form like drops of nectar, squeezed from the flowering of our lives.

Is Your God a Day Late and a $ Short?

Is your God a day late and a $ short? Because mine frequently is, or so it seems.

Although the love of it may be the root of all evil, money keeps the wolf from the door, the bacon on the table, the gas tank filled, and the kids in college.

It is the push that comes to shove us out into the subway on a Monday morning, and the curve that grades the economy—usually by the length of the unemployment lines at one end, and the gold reserves in Fort Knox at the other.

Small may be beautiful, but less is generally not enough. Especially when that less won't pay the mortgage, or keep the lights turned on. One of the reasons we can't take it with us is that by the time we're ready to go, it has already gone—money, that is!

We may extol the virtues of poverty, but from a discreet distance while we pray it stays far away from us. Money may not be able to buy happiness, true; but, unfortunately, happiness cannot buy money. That is what keeps us looking up to God as the arbitrator of all our "haves," "have nots," and "would like to haves."

As one man told me, "I never pray better than when I have just come from making a bank deposit, nor with greater desperation than when I am going to see about a loan. Then I reach almost mystical heights of spiritual intensity and sincerity."

If things don't turn out the way we pray they should, we wag our finger and cluck our tongue at heaven, and sit down to analyze sixteen reasons why.

In our audacity, we put God on trial to defend why nice things happen to nasty people, and nasty things happen to nice people. When nice things happen to nice people, and nasty things happen to nasty people, we are willing to acquit him.

We are also willing to acquit him if the nasty people turn into nice people because of the nice things that have happened to them: but not if the nice people turn into nasty people because of the nasty things that have happened to them.

This leaves God in the middle of a muddle.

The fact of the matter is that when it comes to misfortune we ask, "*Why me,* Lord?" and when it comes to fortune we ask, "*Why not me,* Lord?"

While he was still in high school, my husband poured some of the hard-earned cash he made delivering the morning newspaper into a piece of waterfront property in an isolated spot several miles up the inlet from Vancouver, Canada. The access road was supposed to go in within a couple of years, at which time he predicted a development boom that would make him a fortune.

By the time we were married, some ten years later,

the property was still in its virgin state, well off the beaten path of civilization, with not a road nor development in sight. As an investment it had not done a thing except levy an annual tax on our stringent budget.

John thought I should take a look at it, so one drizzly Wednesday morning, almost a year to the date of our wedding, we rowed out from the dock at North Vancouver.

I have never been able to understand the rationale of a man who would spend hundreds of dollars on a flight north from California and then compromise to the thrift of a row boat ... rather than rent a motor boat, or, for that matter, hire a water taxi that was guaranteed to take us where we wanted to go, pronto, and then pick us up, hopefully in a couple of hours, which, was about the limit of my endurance to being soaking wet.

As I shivered in the stern of the little boat and felt the rain trickle rivulets down the collar of my windbreaker, I was torn between the exhilaration of the exquisite beauty of the Canadian Northwest and the physical discomfort that instantly programmed into my psyche a top priority for central heating and tea, served piping hot and preferably in a bone china cup. I decided there and then that when stretched beyond those two points, my commitment to love withers.

As his strong arms stroked a fast pace, in between huffs and puffs, John described our "dream house." His Pendleton shirt, faded jeans, and logger's boots displayed a physique in top condition. The fresh air, the rhythmic lap of the oars pulling against the water, and the fact that we were alone in the middle of nowhere stirred my primitive juices, and my emotions ran the gamut from lustful pride at being married to a bionic man, and sulky resentment at his attitude that compromised my comfort to a show of his strength.

We clambered onto the slippery bank and faced a steep cliff of insurmountable granite.

"Here it is, home," John beamed, "solid rock. The Bible says to build your house on rock!"

I leaned against the cold grey stone and watched the waves soak my shoes, my socks and the bottom of my slacks. Suddenly I knew the literal meaning of being caught between a rock and a hard place.

"Isn't this terrific?" he glowed.

"Yes," I lied.

The only fresh water was in a stream some three lots over. There was no sign of an access road, no potential electricity, and, what was worse, no sanitation. The dollars and cents value of an investment that he had been dangling before my eyes like a lucrative carrot disintegrated.

It took us over an hour to find a way up the cliff, then another to build a small fire and roast a pack of soggy wieners.

Six hours later, you never saw a woman so happy to get back to a hotel. I nearly kissed the floor as we fell in the door.

A few years later, we were offered quadruple what

John had paid for the lot. I felt it was an act of divine providence, and I groveled in gratitude. John snarled and wondered if we should hold on just a little while longer.

We decided to go to joint and individual prayer. To seek the guidance of God, to whom we had abandoned the direction of our lives, and to whom we had made a commitment of full surrender.

We tried to do everything right.

We searched the scriptures. We trusted in the Lord with all our hearts, and we sought not to lean to our own understanding. In all our ways we acknowledged him, and we expected that he would direct our path. (Proverbs 3:5).

We read James in several versions, and they all told us that if we lacked wisdom, we should ask God, and he would give it to us—liberally. *We did,* and expected that *he would.*

At the end of the week, we both felt an affirmation of the leading of the Holy Spirit. This we reinforced by a practical analysis of our circumstances. The car desperately needed replacing, raising children brought the stress of added financial demands, and the quality of our here and now could be much enhanced by a windfall profit.

God had obviously sent us some stupid buyer with more money than sense. Not feeling a bit sorry for him, but elated at our good fortune, we sold.

Two years later, the housing boom exploded across the North American continent—the lot was worth a hundredfold more; it would not only have bought us a new car, it would have paid off the mortgage on our home as well!

Our God was not a day late, but two years too early—and he was several thousand dollars short.

We felt shortchanged in the prayer line.

The fact that we had indeed made a fairly nice profit on an original small investment seemed irrelevant and trivial when compared to the enormous profit we could have made. We simmered with regret.

About the same time, a friend of ours was caught in between jobs. He had applied for the one he really wanted, out of state. Several months had passed and, despite many follow-through queries, he had not heard from the organization. Then, out of the blue, he was offered a job locally. He felt lukewarm towards it as it was a professional compromise. He had to decide whether to take it or not by the Monday, two weeks from date of the offer.

"My wife and I went to prayer," he said. "We were starting to crunch financially as our back-up reserves were literally being eaten up week by week. Like Gideon, we decided to lay out a fleece before the Lord, and seek his will through a sign."

So he would not misread the signs, Gideon opted for a double check-point: wet wool and dry ground the first night, dry wool and wet ground the second night.

"After putting through yet another query," our friend said, "if I still have no decision on the position I want by the deadline Monday, I will take the local job."

He activated prayer lines around his circle of friends. He asked for the moving of the will of God to guide and override any error in decision made either by organization management, or by himself.

Time passed. Nothing happened.

On the designated Monday, disappointed and disgruntled, but in obedient keeping with the covenant of his fleece, he accepted the local job. Tuesday morning the mail held a letter giving him the out-of-state position he had wanted so badly. His God was *exactly* a day late!

I wish I could say that the local job turned out for the best and all went well to affirm divine guidance, but it didn't. In order to keep the bread on the table he settled down in a business compromise that frustrated his professional goals for many years. Yet he believed, as heartily as Gideon, that he was moving under the authority of the sign of God's guidance.

Was his fleece that of a lesser God?

I have sat through so many prayer meetings where testimonies were shared of how this person asked for $400 and received $900 instead; or that person faithpromised $1,000 and was able to give $2,000 or more; and I have added my glory alleluia and amen to all the wonderful provisions of the Lord. But a part of me has winced.

Several years ago I tried to pull together a house of help for runaway kids in the canyon up the hill from where we live. They were smashed out on drugs, alcohol, or simply crumbling under the anguish of a wrong turn taken in the road map of their lives. For the most part they were not "bad" kids, just prodigals who had not returned home, and the tragedy was that in many cases they were "throw-away" kids and their parents did not want them home.

I asked God for $450 to confirm a lease. He gave me $120, and when I looked up at him startled with disappointment, he chastened my heart, "Before you ask for more, Fay, use what I have put in your hand."

I did, and when it was gone, another hundred dollars trickled in; and when that was gone and I once again offered God my empty hand, he showed me not more money, but talents programmed into that hand so that when donations dwindled creative stewardship could take over.

Together with other empty, willing hands, we worked out a source of long-term funding—a small thrift shop grew and over the years paid thousands of dollars towards the rent of that house of ministry.

We sometimes behave like the little kid who asked God to help him through a test, then sloughed off on his studies. When he got his final grade, he cocked a surprised eyebrow and said, "Thanks a lot, God, I flunked!"

God seldom does for us what he expects us to do for ourselves, or for him.

God is not hoodwinked—he also knows when we use prayer merely as an excuse for our own reluctance to become involved.

Since teaching me that his provision is frequently worked out through the availability of my own two hands, I study hands.

Large gnarled working hands, small trusting hands, garnished hands with long, painted finger nails, sticky chocolate-coated hands, stubby growing hands, sterile surgeon's hands, earth-soiled planting hands, artistic delicate hands, and trembling aged hands.

On my shelf are a pair of bookends—replicas of Albrecht Dürer's *Praying Hands*. These are the most celebrated hands in art.

I always thought they were the artist's conception of the hands of Jesus. But they are not—although, as a carpenter with rough "working hands" those of Jesus probably looked much like Dürer's painting.

Dürer and a young fellow artist, whom some sources name Hans, were struggling to make ends meet. They worked part-time to support themselves and studied art on the side. One day, frustrated by the sheer exhaustion of the effort, Hans proposed that he would work full time so Albrecht could study art full time. Then, after Albrecht had achieved success and sold some paintings, it would be a turnabout and he could support Hans while he studied art full time.

As Hans toiled long and hard as a laborer, Dürer's genius developed and emerged. Finally, the great day came when Albrecht had enough money jingling in his pockets from the sale of his work to reciprocate and support his friend. Hans quit his menial job and picked up his artist's brush—his hands had become calloused and his joints were enlarged and stiff. His fingers were twisted and ruined for the skill necessary to brush the artist's delicate strokes.

Albrecht Dürer was crushed with sorrow. He knew he could never return to Hans the skill he had sacrificed through his laboring hands, but he could give the world a tribute to the nobility of a friend's selfless love.

He painted the working hands, as he had so often seen them, lifted in prayer. He included the broken fingernails, the enlarged joints, and the heavy veins. Around the world the hands of his faithful intercessor and facilitator have become a symbol of prayerful, sacrificial love.

Daily I give my hands to God.

"Work through them, Lord," I pray. "Use them. Get them dirty when other hands may pull back from dirty jobs. Hold, touch, feel through them. Stroke, comfort, heal through them. Pray through them."

Some days he writes through them. On others he simply plucks flowers through them. He washes, scrubs, mends, or pulls weeds through them, and in their menial tasks they are still praying hands, serving him.

God does *not* "expect day labor, light denied."

He *is* God of the impossible; he *is* hope of the hopeless. When we are powerless to help ourselves, or when no one is able to help us, God moves his miracles through our lives.

The stars fill the African night with the brightness of endless galaxies visible in few other places in the world. As diamonds in the firmament they wink through the majesty of trillions of light years to aura the imagination of man and catch him in breathless wonder at the infinite power of creation.

"I stood on the verandah of the hospital," the doctor told me, "looking into the African night. I gripped the rail with both my hands as the tears poured down my cheeks. I searched the heavens to find the face of God."

In the telling of the memory, the tears once again spilled down his cheeks and he paused as words choked in his throat.

He had completed a surgery in the small mission station, and the man lay dying for lack of blood. Wedded to his calling with a passion that held in sacred trust the sanctity of God-given life, he was more than doctor, missionary, friend, or even saint. He was a scalpel curved against the palm of God.

"I have no blood," he cried. "You fed four thousand with seven loaves; you turned water into wine. . . . Fill this man's veins tonight!"

"Suddenly," he said, "I felt an arm around my shoulders—a heavy weighted arm that gripped me with a fierce strength that nearly spun me round about. Surprised, I looked behind me. There was no one there, yet I continued to feel that arm. A strange expectation filled my heart and my pulse quickened. Slowly I found myself walking back to surgery. There I saw my patient, with the rosy glow of life."

God took the miracle of that doctor's skill, the miracle of his heart's compassion, and the miracle of his faith in asking, to perform the miracle of his divine intervention.

"Not all my patients are so supernaturally saved,"

the doctor grinned, "but I never cease to feel that arm around my shoulders—his continual presence, that is my miracle!"

We are so programmed to the hype of the sensational that our spiritual eyes dim at the simplicity of the legacy that is our daily miracle.

The indwelling presence of the Holy Spirit, making intercession for us in all our infirmities; the intensity of the love of Jesus that gives and gives and gives; the mercy of his grace which promises to be our all sufficiency; and the awesome vulnerability of God, who laid the foundations of the earth and created light to break the darkness, in bending and limiting himself to our asking . . . the miracle of prayer.

R. A. Torrey said, "Prayer is the only omnipotence that God has granted to man—the power of prayer is the power of God.

Rule one of prayer is PRAY. Moment by moment, word by stumbling word, hesitantly or confidently, audibly or silently, God hears the whispers of our hearts. Sometimes it is a sigh—sometimes it is a scream.

Thinking about it is not praying; talking about it is not praying; reading about it is not praying; only praying is praying!

If we pray in faith, believing—good. If we pray, swimming in a sea of doubts, and fan a smoldering flax of hope—good.

I am embarrassed by the number of prayers I have falteringly, casually, flippantly, doubtingly, or even resentfully sent up to heaven, and in the unconditional love of his infinite mercy, looking through the frailty of my faith to the needs of my transparent heart, God has blessed those prayers.

So often I feel like the man who attended a Kathryn Kuhlman service. He watched with simmering doubt the crutches and wheel chairs set aside and radiant faces aglow with the healing power of God until he could bear it no longer. Putting his hand on a tumor the size of a walnut on his neck, he cried in desperation, "Hell, God—I need to be healed!" He felt the tumor leave, and the softness of his neck malleable to his hand.

Like the man, blind from birth, whom Jesus healed with clay moistened in spit (of all things!)... "One thing I know," he said, "that whereas I was blind, now I see" (John 9:25).

We tremble in wonder.

Then I am amazed at the times I am spiritually tuned—I have confessed my sins, forgiven those who have trespassed against me, and prayed a prayer of faith expecting the dynamic of an immediate answer ... and I wait, and wait with no evident response.

It is our prerogative to ask; it is God's prerogative to answer. Jesus said, "*You* do the asking, *I* will do the answering." We resource the fullness of our opportunity, but dare not pit the perspective of our finite vision against the infinite wisdom of divinity, who works out his most perfect will in the lives of those who trust him. We rest in that trust and pray ... without ceasing!

The disciples asked, "Lord teach us how to pray."

Jesus could so easily have given a six-part seminar on effective spiritual communication; or a ten-point outline on the helps and hazards of breaking through the human sound barrier to bend the ear of God.

He didn't.

Instead, he gave us the example of a prayer—two verses, some fifty-eight words short. They affect our lives and are the best of all possible places to start: "Our Father, who art in heaven . . ."

I like to pray, "*My* Father, who is in heaven . . ." or, when praying for my children, "Ian's Father, who is in heaven, teach him to hallow your name, bring your kingdom into life, give him yourself as his bread of life, and forgive him his sins . . ." and so forth.

Rule two of prayer is PRAY. When all nerve endings are short-circuiting, DON'T PANIC—PRAY! A friend of mine gives out little cards with that simple message.

After giving out hundreds of the cards on one particularly difficult day, she decided, "Prayer doesn't seem to be working, I think I'll try panic!"

She reversed her card to its blank side up on her refrigerator door, and she let loose. She snapped at those around her; she cried at her dilemmas; she groaned at the hurts that assailed her. She yelled and screamed and carried on.

Her husband came home, took one look, and said, "Well, you've finally gone bonkers!"

"It was the worst day of my life," she moaned. "Panic doesn't work, I tried it. Better stay with PRAY." She turned her message card back to its rightful position and ordered several hundred more.

Rule three of prayer is PRAY. It is not the position of the body but the condition of the heart that counts. We can stand on our heads and twiddle our toes and pray, and God will still hear us.

How lovely it is when our environment lends itself to prayer—those long walks in the woods, or sitting on a hillside with cool breezes caressing our hair. It is easy to feel the presence of God at times like those. I pray in the bathtub. Sometimes I shut my eyes and pretend that I am sitting on a hillside and I can almost feel the crisp breeze, only to realize that it is just the bath water getting cold and I had better shake a leg and flick a towel before I get pneumonia.

I pray when I am brushing my teeth. I have even prayed in the middle of making love—I thank God for kisses and that it was nice of him to program pleasure points into our bodies. He didn't have to!

I pray in the middle of a crowd when noise and clutter makes thinking hardly possible. I also pray in the quiet of the middle of the night when the silence amplifies every pounding thought.

The only *rule of prayer is* PRAY. Without circumventing scriptural directionals, encouragements, and admonitions (and there are many), the bottom line of prayer is to PRAY. When we do, the power of heaven picks up momentum to change our lives.

Much as we try to put him there, God is not on trial; the good news is that neither is man. Jesus Christ stood in the docket on our behalf.

If the answers to our prayers depended upon our

worth, they would never be answered—they would never even be heard. Through the righteousness of Christ, they are.

We tend to stroke *prayer* like a lucky rabbit's foot, and seek God's fleece rather than his face.

We try to manipulate his will to ours and sometimes call it faith. We push forward in the arrogance of our own stoic determination, limited by our finite vision, rather than pull back in the simple trust of his infinite plan.

We expect him to change the sovereignty of his omnipotent heart, instead of humbly asking him to give us a heart willing to be changed.

"Be still and know that I am God" (Psalm 46:10) means, "Relax, let God be God!"

I thank God for the prayers he has answered the way I prayed that he would.

I thank him, somewhat shamefully, for the prayers I prayed and then forgot all about; but he didn't, and in his lovingkindness he answered them anyway.

I also thank God for the prayers he didn't answer the way I prayed he would; I shudder to think of how some things in my life may have turned out if he had!

In the mystery of his timing, in the confusion where I do not understand—God is God. I will not diagnose him, I will not analyze him. I will obey him, I will adore him, and I will continue to lay my life before him.

The priorities of prayer are:

His Person—then his promise.
His Presence—then his provision
His Praise—then his power

This puts into perspective the "have," "have not," and "would like to have" of our life.

David Olson of World Vision writes, "God must have heard (and often turned down) millions of requests for ten speed bikes, nice weather, toothache relief, sexier figures, job promotions, and chances for a house in a prestigious neigborhood. Has He heard as many requests for a heart like Christ's, a mind like His, an eye for the lost, an ear to the needy, or ready hands?"

The intercourse of our spirit made one with his, prayer is the intimate communication of a love that should breathe through our every breath, pulse through our every heartbeat, and knit us to divinity.

When we delight ourselves in the Lord, through his *Person*, his *Presence*, and his *Praise* (Glory), we are enabled to say with Brother Lawrence:

"I know not what God purposes with me, or keeps me for; I am in a calm so great that I fear naught. What can I fear when I am with Him; and with Him, in His Presence, I hold myself the most I can. May *all things* Praise Him!"